THE AMERICAN SEXUAL DILEMMA

THE AMERICAN SEXUAL DILEMMA

Edited by WILLIAM L. O'NEILL
Rutgers University

HOLT, RINEHART AND WINSTON, INC.
New York • Chicago • San Francisco • Atlanta
Dallas • Montreal • Toronto • London • Sydney

Cover photograph by Dick Swift.

CONTENTS

"We want to report a stolen car." *(The Granger Collection)*

INTRODUCTION

Few topics have aroused more interest than changing sexual norms, and fewer are more difficult to analyze historically. Statistics on divorce rates, age at marriage, average number of children and the like tell us something about what went on, but sexual behavior remains for the most part private, and hence nearly inaccessible. Happily, there are signs of change that a historian can read, if imperfectly. What people say and write about sex has some value. Observed and recorded behavior is useful too. What is thought immoral at any given time can be compared with definitions of immorality at other times. And since the 1920s there have been scientific studies of increasing accuracy which provide more clues. Thus, while much remains to be learned, and a great deal will probably never be known about American sexuality over time, we can now at least approach the subject. So far there has been little historical writing on the period after 1929, so that we must still rely primarily on journalists and social scientists for information. Yet, despite obvious differences in method and intent, there is enough congruence among the students of sexuality to make possible a book of readings such as this.

Although experts differ on how extensively sexual standards have changed, and even more on what these changes mean, there is a rough consensus on certain points. Most agree that something we may call a sexual revolution has been taking place among the middle class and that it appears to consist mainly of an increase in feminine promiscuity and a decline in censorship and the policing of morals. Little is known about lower-class sexuality. The upper class (as distinct from the merely rich) is too small and discreet to be examinable. Our ignorance about these classes is serious though not fatal since it is the middle class that has most to do with setting national standards in taste and behavior.

The revolution in middle-class morals first became manifest after World War I. But as with all great changes there were early signs of what was to come. During the period 1912–1917, as Henry F. May has shown, traditional American culture was breaking down and modern cultural patterns were beginning to take shape. Sexual freedom did not, therefore, grow in a vacuum. Rather it was intimately linked to even more profound disturbances that were creating the world we live in now. Of course domestic behavior has its own wellsprings that are not closely tied to the general culture. Divorce, for example, had been on the rise since early in the nineteenth century and continued to afterwards. On the

1

whole it seems to have been only marginally affected by events in society at large. By the same token since at least 1860 the age of marriage for both men and women has been increasing, while average family size has declined—save only for a short period from the mid-1940s to the late 1950s when both trends were reversed. These are examples of profound social movements that are not usually responsive to outside pressure.

Sexual behavior appears somewhat more variable. So far as we can tell sexual repression increased through the nineteenth century, then declined in the twentieth, most strikingly in the 1920s, for reasons that are as yet far from clear. Henry F. May argues that the demand for and practice of sexual freedom, and the fear thus aroused, were "cracks in the surface" of a failing culture. James R. McGovern, on the other hand, is concerned with the economic and technological developments affecting women before World War I. As he points out, these changes were impressive. The first decade of the century saw a sharp increase in the employment of women. The mechanization of housework enabled women to leave the home for greater periods of time. Social norms were modified to encourage women to take part in recreations and associations formerly denied them. Technology and ideology conspired to form a new image of women which reflected to some extent a new reality.

A few caveats are in order here. The pre-war changes were limited chiefly to upper-middle-class women. Although many more women worked after 1900 than before, most toiled for very low wages. Not only shop and factory girls, but secretaries and even school teachers made too little money to buy the products and enjoy the pleasures described by McGovern. But the small minority of vanguard women were important all the same because they represented a new style of life that was to spread rapidly after the war. The trends they started would soon move outward to embrace larger numbers of women, especially young women. Thus, while it is important to know that much of what made the 1920s distinctive existed earlier, it is also vital to remember that it was not until the twenties that the new feminine life style was broadly established. This delay was caused in part by the time it takes for high status innovations to filter down, and partly because the new life styles depended on a degree of affluence and leisure that relatively few people enjoyed until after the war. Only then were incomes high enough, and the work week short enough, for substantial numbers to indulge themselves as here described. Is McGovern right in saying that historians ought properly to trace the revolution in morals from before World War I? Or is it more usefully examined when at its peak in the 1920s?

In one way or another all the contributors to this volume are concerned with the great transition experienced by developed countries from the industrial to the post-industrial era, from the age of production to the age of consumption. Before industrialization the great mass of men were preoccupied with survival, business chiefly with the problems of production. Once these basic hurdles were leaped and a high level of productivity achieved business became more and more involved with the problems of consumption. People had more money to spend, and it became the great goal of business to persuade them to part with it. The jazz age was, therefore, in part at least a moment when the wants of people and the needs of business coincided. Nearly all the social and ideological influences discussed in this volume impelled men and especially women to want more freedoms and new pleasures. They were able to act on their impulses because the economy permitted it and business demanded it.

Post-industrial society is based on hedonism, an ethic promoted by advertising and the mass media. What work was to the old era play is to the new. Businessmen continued for generations to pay lip service to the ancient virtues of hard work, discipline, and self-denial, but in practice they encouraged the pleasure principle because that was what moved goods. Inevitably, sexual pleasure became part of the new order. It could be sold directly in books, films, and a variety of entertainments. Indirectly it could be used to sell a host of other products from toothpaste to automobiles in ways that soon became all too familiar. Again, it must be remembered that many Americans never shared in the new order. Though incomes were high enough in the 1920s to launch the postindustrial society they were not sufficient to sustain it; hence the crash. Even at its peak the great boom left perhaps a majority of Americans still engaged in the struggle for survival. Yet a sizable fraction of the populace did enter the age of mass consumption, and though interrupted by depression and another war, they formed the basis of American life as it exists today.

William E. Leuchtenburg's description of life in the jazz age will appear strange, exotic, or alien only to the reader who cannot substitute current songs, books, movie titles, and the like for old ones. Past fashions by definition seem passé, but what Leuchtenburg writes of is our own society in embryo. It was a time when the mass media had come to dominate popular culture, when entertainers had national followings, when one dance rage followed the other, when sexuality was constantly under discussion or on exhibit, and so on. The cult of youth which has dominated every prosperous time since then was well-developed. Why this should be so is hard to explain. Though we take it for granted that youth is the best and most admired time of life, the generations before 1900 rarely did. Is there perhaps a necessary connection between hedonism and youth, or do we only imagine it?

Although the flapper was only one feature of the age, much about the new era can be learned from examining her as the thoughtful essay by Kenneth A. Yellis shows. It is especially useful for establishing the subtle links between the image of woman, her clothing, and the economic institutions concerned with these matters. The flapper was herself a transient, or perhaps transitional, figure in the evolution of womankind. But many of her attributes, the demand for personal freedom, devotion to the pleasure principle, and present-mindedness as against planning for the more distant future, have become more or less permanent. The challenge she posed to the merchandisers of fashion has been repeated time and again since the 1920s, and never more so than in the 1960s when the classic skirt-length controversy was re-enacted with surprisingly few variations from the original script.

Professor Leuchtenburg's essay concludes with an apt warning on the consequences of the revolution in morals that echoes the concern of Charlotte Perkins Gilman. No single woman had done more than she to destroy the Victorian stereotype of femininity. Few struggled harder to achieve freedom, and self-development, and to contribute usefully to society. Her stream of books, essays, poems, and stories all aimed to awaken women to their possibilities and to demand the opportunity to grow and serve. Like many older feminists she was appalled to discover after 1920 that comparatively few women, especially younger women, shared her values. For good reasons and bad they turned their backs on the ethic of work, self-denial, discipline, sacrifice, and service that had motivated generations of other women activists. Some did so because the great work now seemed to have been done, others because the opportunities gained appeared less real and satisfying than had been expected. It was possible for women to work at jobs once closed to them. It was still very hard to juggle the rival claims of family and career, or even when committed to professions to rise very high in them. At the same time the pleasure principle competed with the old ethic, even after marriage. The simple role of housewife, discredited to an extent by feminism, was rehabilitated and endowed with new charms. The mechanized outward-looking home was thought to be more challenging and rewarding than the old. The new woman was supposed to be capable of remaining young and beautiful after marriage as her mother had not been. And thanks to the revolution in morals she was to have a stimulating sex life that added a whole new level of experience to domesticity.

To Mrs. Gilman this seemed regressive, a throwback to the Victorian habit of exploiting women's sexuality. For decades she had argued that the Victorian ideal forced women to become sex objects by denying them other means of accomplishment and satisfaction. Middle-class Victorian women may not have had rich sex lives, as they were shielded from contact with the erotic where possible. But as marriage was the whole purpose of their lives they were made to prepare for it by becoming ultrafeminine in the sense of dressing and behaving entirely to please men. Fashion proved the point by emphasizing their breasts and hips and sometimes, as with the bustle, even their buttocks. Mrs. Gilman wanted women to free themselves from this stultifying and degrading role. When instead they merely revised it to broaden their sphere of operations and enlarge their sexual potential, Mrs. Gilman feared that much of what had been gained for women would be lost. Was Mrs. Gilman right? Is an emphasis on feminine sexuality always exploitive of women? Has sexual freedom in truth made women freer? Happier?

From the twenties to the sixties, however, people did not worry about the role of women but only about the much narrower question of their sexual behavior. In the thirties even this attracted relatively little interest by comparison with the economic and political issues that dominated the era. Still, a few studies were made by social scientists, the great Kinsey project was begun, and Dorothy D. Bromley and Florence H. Britten examined the sex lives of college students. Their method was to send questionnaires to selected schools, of which 1,364 from men and women at forty-six colleges and universities were returned. They supplemented the questionnaires with several hundred personal interviews. Though hardly a scientific sample, its results compared favorably with the much larger and more reliable Kinsey study. Like Kinsey, Bromley and Britten found that among upper-middle-class youth, half the men and a quarter of the women had had intercourse by the age of twenty. They also found that about 64 percent of the women were prepared in principle to have intercourse under the right circumstances, which meant usually when in love.

In the chapter reprinted here Bromley and Britten attempt to account for the sexual norms they were to explore in such detail through the rest of the book. This effort is as interesting for its strengths as for its weaknesses. They are frequently on solid ground, as when discussing the automobile, the mass media, the lengthening of adolescence, and other elements facilitating youthful sexuality. But they also express the conventional liberal wisdom of the day which was frequently questionable. Everyone insisted, as many still do, that the family was being weakened, perhaps destroyed, by changing customs. The divorce rate kept going up, children did not emulate their parents, no one spent any time at home. Yet even now with the divorce rate rising once more and sex even freer, the marriage rate has risen too. The proportion of adults who marry, usually for life, is higher now than at any time. And most who divorce remarry again. Their complaint is not with marriage and the family, only with their particular situation. Is it fair to say, then, that the family system is collapsing? That it has changed seems clear enough. But do these changes mean decline or growth, or something else altogether? Nor is the intimate connection between industrialization and changing morals quite so obvious as it seemed to Bromley and Britten. Most women who worked in factories were not themselves emancipated. Even now do most women who work become emancipated thereby? What have been the actual effects of women's work on women's lives? Bromley and Britten took for granted what still needs analyzing. All the same, they were able to describe how the new standards of feminine sexual behavior had been integrated into college life. There would be relatively little change thereafter until at least the mid-sixties. The number employing these norms would keep growing as the percentage of Americans who went to college and became middle class grew.

Most of the early sex studies were either too unscientific or based on inadequate samples. All the same, much can be learned from them. Katherine B. Davis in *Factors In The Sex Life Of 2,200 Women* established the values and practices of older, college-educated women. Gilbert V. T. Hamilton studied two hundred married people in depth for his *A Research on Marriage*. In the 1930s Lewis M. Terman refined the new scientific techniques for his *Pychological Factors in Marital Happiness*. These and other efforts paved the way for Alfred C. Kinsey and his associates, who made the most ambitious efforts to explain American sexuality, especially in two notable works *Sexual Behavior in the Human Male* (1948) and *Sexual Behavior in the Human Female* (1953). Kinsey was a noted zoologist at the University of Indiana who was inspired to begin his great work by discovering, when preparing to give a course on sex education, that too little was known about sexual behavior to properly discuss it. Unlike other sex researchers Kinsey was a taxonomist who had observed and classified enormous numbers of insects. This prepared him to deal with human sexual behavior on the scale needed to achieve something like accuracy. His own goal was for the group to record 100,000 interviews, and though he died before it could be reached the two basic studies had over 12,000 lengthy interviews to draw on. Kinsey did not obtain a true cross section of the American people. Like most such investigations his was weighted toward college-educated, middle-class, whites living in the northeast. But his sample was more comprehensive than any other as to both age and class and provided data of incomparable worth.

Each profession found different things of value in the Kinsey reports. Sociologists were struck by the difference class made in sexual behavior. So much so in fact that future mobility could be predicted from sexual behavior. Thus, a lower-class boy who masturbated regularly had an assured future. But a middle-class boy who fornicated was already downwardly mobile. In this manner was the great bourgeois principle of delayed gratification, the very keystone of the capitalist ethic, justified by science.

For historians two aspects of the Kinsey report are probably of most interest. First, Kinsey evaluated his subjects by age and established that women born after 1900 did indeed have significantly more pre-marital sexual experience than women born earlier. The other intriguing aspect of the Kinsey reports is how people received them, the study of men, especially, since it appeared first and aroused the most controversy. Both reports were major cultural events. When the first volume hit the best-seller lists it was called the "K-bomb." Publication date of the second was proclaimed "K-day" in headlines by newspapers around the country. Delegates to the Republican national convention in 1948 wore buttons reading "We want Kinsey, the people's choice." A regional survey found that the first Kinsey report was better known than the Marshall Plan. Much of the response, particularly from ministers, politicians, and psychiatrists, was negative. But as Erdman Palmore discovers, the other professions concerned with sexual behavior generally welcomed Kinsey's work. The furor surrounding both reports showed that sexual liberation, such as it then was, had clearly not reduced the public interest in sex at all. Most subsequent events in the history of sex would demonstrate this point also. But when the din subsided Kinsey's work remained largely intact. Apart from their intrinsic value, Kinsey's reports established sex research as a legitimate and important field of scientific research and paved the way for William H. Masters and Virginia E. Johnson, among others, who came later.

This acclaim does not mean that Kinsey's serious critics can be disregarded. The weakness in Kinsey's work was not so much a matter of technical defects, though there were some, as in the assumptions, frequently contradictory and usually unstated, which guided his work. Lionel Trilling's brilliant essay on Kinsey makes this abundantly clear. Trilling is not, of course, without his own prejudices. Thus he criticizes Kinsey for not showing more respect for the Freudian belief that women experience two kinds of orgasm—clitoral and vaginal. This was an important theme in Freudian literature, for which there was practically no physiological evidence and which Masters and Johnson would later crushingly disprove. Trilling is perhaps on firmer ground in thinking Kinsey's view of the male inability to sustain intercourse was oversimplified. But here too Masters and Johnson were to have much success in curing men of premature ejaculation with rather simple behavioral conditioning. Still, sexuality is far too complex and even now too little understood to make the Kinsey attitudes which Trilling exposes defensible. The tendency of much sex research is to reduce human sexuality to an essentially mechanical, largely harmless enterprise that finds expression in countless morally neutral ways. This is what might be expected in an age of technocratic liberalism. It is surely better than the witless enthusiasm of contemporary sexual radicals who are persuaded that orgasm makes you free. But is it good enough now when several generations of sexual freedom have failed to noticeably improve the human condition? Or, as some think, is the problem still that sex is not free enough?

In some respects the Masters and Johnson experience seemed to duplicate Kinsey's. In both cases the publication of scientific research into sex caused a sensation. Both groups wrote two basic books that were quickly celebrated. But comparisons cannot be carried much further than this. Masters and Johnson had a much easier time of it than Kinsey. Though there were the usual complaints from psychiatrists, ministers, and moral conservatives, Masters and Johnson experienced very little serious negative criticism. For one thing, the work they did was much more immediately verifiable than Kinsey's. Where Kinsey had only asked people how they behaved sexually, Masters and Johnson observed them under laboratory conditions. The result was a body of physiological data that other scientists could duplicate. They found it overwhelmingly persuasive. Masters and Johnson also prepared the medical and scientific community for what was to come. In a series of papers and meetings they gradually disclosed the nature of their work and what they had learned from it to fellow scientists before the general public was informed. When published in *Human Sexual Response* and *Human Sexual Inadequacy* their work enjoyed the approbation of medical science and this enormously hastened its acceptance. Then too, times had changed since Kinsey—partly in fact because of Kinsey. Sex research was no longer viewed with such suspicion. Attitudes had become distinctly more liberal. Thus, like Kinsey, Masters and Johnson proved something about sexuality as a public issue in addition to enlarging our understanding of sex itself.

Approval was not, however, as Fred Belliveau and Lin Richter indicate, unanimous. Perhaps the single most effective attack on Masters and Johnson was by Leslie H. Farber. The appearance of his essay forced Masters and Johnson to advance their publication date in self-defense. It also raised questions that are fundamental not only to sex as a field of research, but to the whole American approach to sexuality. This is not to say that Farber was entirely right. He knew too little about the project, at the time he wrote, to judge it fairly. He thought it chiefly concerned with female masturbation when in fact the whole range of genital activity was at issue. He denigrates the need to know complete physical truth about copulation and orgasm. He reflects the usual psychiatric prejudice against sex research which involves at least some envy and some fear that psychoanalysis will be undercut.

All the same, as Trilling had pointed out earlier, there are limits to what can be learned from science and technology. The American attempt to substitute mechanics for philosophy here, though consistent with the national culture, is both pathetic and to a degree self-defeating. Where once women were taught to fear having sex, they now fear not having it, or more precisely not having an orgasm. And men are afraid also, for where once their pleasure was the test of successful intercourse now their partner's pleasure is the badge of mastery. This represents an ethical advance if nothing else. Yet it is not at all clear that the sum total of sexual anxiety has been much reduced in consequence. Sexual behavior continues to be mysterious, baffling, and uncertain despite all that sex research has done to lay bare the facts.

The next two selections underscore this point. The Commission on Pornography and Obscenity takes what might be called the common sense approach to their subject. As against the folk wisdom on pornography (summed up by one dissenting commissioner who wrote that the American people know that "one who wallows in filth is going to get dirty"), most commissioners decided on the basis of certain studies that sexual patterns are essentially stable and not much affected by pornography one way or another. The problem then reduces itself to the question of shielding minors, and that part of the public hostile to pornography, from exposure to it.

Irving Kristol, on the other hand, holds views that are at once more extreme and more profound than the commission's, though not necessarily more correct. He rejects both folk wisdom and what is now the conventional wisdom of liberals in favor of what might be termed a classically conservative position. Conservatives believe that what has worked reasonably well over time ought to be sustained unless overwhelming evidence against it can be marshaled. More specifically, Kristol thinks that sexual behavior and social well-being are related to the extent that one cannot at the same time have both a good society and a totally uncensored one. He implies that as fifty years of steadily expanding sexual freedom have failed to materially advance the public welfare the time has come for the burden of proof to rest on those who demand even fewer restraints than now exist.

The debate over pornography for reasons of space must here represent those other sexual topics which still arouse controversy—contraception, abortion, and the like. Each has it friends and foes, but in general the arguments have not developed much in the last half century for all the apparent behavioral changes that have taken place. The majority of adult Americans, contrary often to their own practice when young, believe that only a few of the sexual possibilities open to humanity are legitimate. Liberals continue to feel that most sexual possibilities are at least morally and socially neutral in their consequences, if not actually positive. A much smaller group, represented here especially by Trilling, Farber, and Kristol, reject both positions in favor of complex and often highly personal alternatives. As there is no way of reconciling these differences the best way of ending these readings is with John Corry's sober, objective review of what seemed to be the actual behavior of Americans in the 1960s.

In the reprinted selections footnotes appearing in the original sources have in general been omitted unless they contribute to the argument or better understanding of the selection.

HENRY F. MAY (b. 1915) is Professor of American History at the University of California at Berkeley. Here he describes the moral code of genteel Americans in the early twentieth century and explains some of the social and intellectual forces that would soon destroy it.*

Henry F. May

Changing Ideas

Young Intellectuals constantly attacked Puritanism; actually, nineteenth-century Anglo-Americans were stricter about sexual morality than their Puritan ancestors. Liberal religion, giving less emphasis than its predecessors to the theological virtues, gave more to some kinds of conduct. In 1912 religious liberals, respectable freethinkers of the Ingersoll kind, and staunch evangelical Christians still saw eye to eye about sexual morality.

Chastity was, whether by divine precept or common consent, as absolute a good as honesty, and (this was tacitly admitted) far more difficult. Not all Americans agreed with Billy Sunday about the reality of a personal devil, but most had reason to believe in temptation. Paradox

lay at the root of the matter: sexual intercourse in marriage was a sacred duty, romantic love the most beautiful thing in life, and sexual lust evil. Since women, except the depraved few, were naturally pure, it was best that they have jurisdiction over the whole field of sexual relations. The duty of men was to make every effort to grow up pure, and especially to avoid the debilitating dangers that arose from evil thoughts. The crown of the whole civilization was the American family, with the father supreme in the economic sphere but the mother, freer and more respected than the women of other countries, in special charge of morals.

The millions of people who believed

*From *The End of American Innocence,* by Henry F. May. Copyright © 1959 by Henry F. May. Reprinted by permission of Alfred A. Knopf, Inc.

in this code and tried to live by it knew of course that it was continually broken. Lapses could be forgiven; outright defiance was far more serious. From Shelley to Sarah Bernhardt distinguished foreigners had flouted the code; now there were Americans who openly repudiated the customs of their own country. The mores of the Luhan circle, the noble and impractical sexual theories of the anarchists, the emancipated attitude of Dell and his friends were only beginning to receive wide circulation. Every now and then a member of the conservative middle class discovered that some people actually advocated and practiced what sounded to him like sheer deliberate wickedness. He was not surprised when such people turned out to be avant-garde artists or writers.

Women's rights were sometimes a corollary of nineteenth century moral progress, yet some kinds of militant feminism could be disturbing. To some American males it was disquieting in itself to find the weaker sex taking on the roles of athlete, professional, or political agitator. Sexual defensiveness was not far below the surface of some of the ridicule directed against allegedly mannish feminists and their effeminate male defenders.

One of the most logical ends of female equality, and one of the most disturbing, was the demand that women take control of their own most important function: childbirth. In 1913 Margaret Sanger, according to her own account, coined the term birth control for a movement that had a long subterranean history. Mrs. Sanger was not hard to connect with the rebellious intellectuals. She had been brought up a socialist and influenced by Emma Goldman, she had contributed to the enlightenment of Mrs. Dodge, and she had summered at Provincetown. Yet

she was inescapably respectable, the wife of an architect and the mother of two children. Her interest in the problem had begun in a way the period approved. As a nurse in the New York slums, she had been horrified by abortion, the death of mothers, and the neglect of children, just as other reformers of the period had been horrified by tenement sanitation.

On her lecture tours, in her editorial and clinical work, and during her trial and imprisonment in 1916 Mrs. Sanger obviously ran into a complex whirlpool of public emotions. Expressions of horror and outrage were many; to some her purpose seemed an almost unbelievable apology for lust. Yet there was clearly another side. Many respectable feminists shared her view that motherhood must not be brought about by uncontrolled male passion, and some sociologists believed that the poorer classes at least must be helped to restrict their offspring. Mrs. Sanger's admirers extended far beyond the desperate and frantic women from the slums who saw her as a personal deliverer from slavery and death. The press noticed that limousines drew up outside her Western lectures. The government, goaded by Comstock and others into persecution, handled Mrs. Sanger with obvious gingerliness and timidity.

Dangerous thoughts about birth and marriage were not the whole trouble; the statistics too were alarming. Since 1867 the national birthrate and the average size of families had been declining. As an endless succession of books and pamphlets was pointing out, the decline was sharpest among the well educated, especially those of native New England stock. Divorce was going up. In 1914 the number of divorces first reached a round hundred thousand. This meant about one per thousand in the population; in 1867 the rate had been .35; in 1920 it was to reach 1.6. President Roosevelt, who had frequently denounced divorce in the press, considered the national sin of "wilful sterility" and the menace of "race suicide" serious enough as early as 1905 to give them considerable space in a message to Congress.[1]

Here too public emotions were divided. It was, after all, a progressive era, and a large and respectable minority thought the family should change with the times. Many sociologists, a sprinkling of liberal ministers, and several of the muckraking magazines agreed that marriage itself needed overhauling. This was the message of William E. Carson's *The Marriage Revolt*, a popular summary of liberal doctrine published in 1915. To Carson the divorce rate and the wide uneasiness about marriage did not mean a spread of evil ideas. It meant that people were finally learning to see marriage not as an unchanging ordinance, but as a custom that could be altered for human happiness. To real moral conservatives, no suggestion could have been more shocking.

The sharpest indication of sexual malaise was the white-slave panic, which reached its unaccountably hysterical peak in the peaceful prewar year 1913. It apparently started with the muckrakers, who had turned to the enticing subject of prostitution as early as 1907. Their attitude was a familiar one: the "Daughters of the Poor" were innocent victims; the real criminals were members of a secret, mysterious white-slave trust. In 1910 Congress attacked this trust with the Mann Act, designed to end the interstate white-slave trade. In the same year the

New York Grand Jury, with John D. Rockefeller as foreman, started an investigation, and in 1911 the Chicago Vice Commission issued its famous report. Within three or four years most of the nation's states and cities conducted some sort of inquiry.

Inevitably, the cause was taken up by sensationalists on the borderline between evangelism, muckraking, and pornography in a number of lurid books about "The Girl Who Disappears." Novelists seized on the subject; the movies devoted a number of full length features to "The Traffic in Souls." Any girl, it seemed, who said hello to a stranger in a large city was likely to be pricked with a poisoned needle and spirited away. She would wake up, helpless, in the brothels of Rio or Constantinople. A correspondent of the *New York World* said that his wife believed fifty thousand women disappeared from Chicago and New York every year, and that more than half the men in the country were working night and day in an organization more formidable than the Steel Trust. Frederick C. Howe, Wilson's liberal Commissioner of Immigration, found himself on Ellis Island the custodian of hundreds of alien men and women, seized on flimsy evidence as prostitutes or procurers. Howe, describing the excitement later, compared it in intensity to the Pro-German hysteria of 1918 and the Red Scare of 1919–20.[2]

By 1913 and 1914, when the panic reached its height, a counteroffensive got under way. Mencken, among others, jumped with delight on this new, superb example of Puritan gullibility. Sober newspapers assured their readers that the poisoned needle was a myth. In a

[1] Fifth Annual Message, December 5, 1905, J. D. Richardson, Comp.: *Messages and Papers of the Presidents* (Washington, 1910), XIV, 7048. See also Roosevelt's *Autobiography* (New York, 1913), pp. 176–184 for discussion of this and similar subjects.

[2] Howe: *Confessions of a Reformer,* pp. 272–88. The *World* reporter's statement is discussed in *Current Opinions,* LVI (1914), 129.

strange backwash of emotions, the censors started to object to white-slave films and novels. In 1913 *Current Opinion,* seizing a phrase of William Marion Reedy's, lamented that it seemed to have struck "Sex O'Clock" in America. Our reticence about sex was yielding, it said, to a frankness that would have startled Paris, and the center of the trouble was the constant discussion of prostitution.[3]

All these and other fears lay behind the reaction of conservative America to the essentially innocent ideas of the Rebellion, and to its favorite literature. No literate American could manage by the mid-teens to ignore Ibsen, Wells, and Dreiser entirely. To many, the solution seemed simple, to tighten the existing censorship. The *Dial,* in 1912, four years before it deserted to the rebels, stated exactly the point of view that the Freudians and others found most abhorrent:

Now reticence may possibly go too far, but no sane person can deny that there are ugly things in life that had better be kept in the dark corners of consciousness.[4]

Ever since the seventies, Anthony Comstock, for one, had been trying to keep them there, and his activities seemed to be reaching a wild crescendo just before his death in 1915. Armed with the federal and state laws which his efforts had secured, commissioned as a special agent by the Post Office Department, backed by his own New York Society for the Suppression of Vice and a network of similar societies in other states, Comstock was a formidable figure. Since he believed deeply in the pervasive, infectious power of evil thoughts, Comstock drew no lines between deliberate pornography, European classic art, and factual reports of

vice commissions. In 1912 he attacked and made famous a painfully decorous picture which had won the medal of honor at the Paris Spring Salon; it was called "September Morning." In 1914 he went after the February issue of the *Chautauquan,* which had on its cover a photograph of a Greek faun recently dug up by a University of Pennsylvania expedition.

To publishers, and especially to new, daring, and vulnerable publishers, Comstock was not by any means a laughing matter, and neither was his slightly less spectacular successor as Secretary of the New York Society, John S. Sumner. Those who defied him might find their books denied the mails and boycotted by booksellers, themselves in court facing an inflamed and hostile jury. In 1913 Comstock led a dramatic raid on Mitchell Kennerley's office and brought the publisher to trial over the novel *Hagar Revelly.* In December 1915 Knopf, barely started, was threatened with attack over Przybyszewski's *Homo Sapiens.* In 1917 Sumner attacked Appleton for publishing *Susan Lenox,* the famous, impeccably uplifting, white-slave novel of the muckraking novelist David Graham Phillips.

The climax of prewar censorship battles, and the prelude to many celebrated engagements of the twenties, raged round the battered head of Theodore Dreiser. In July 1916 the Western Society for the Prevention of Vice, aroused by a Cincinnati minister, attacked *The Genius,* got it removed from the bookstores, secured a temporary cessation-of-circulation order from the Post Office Department and filed a complaint with its New York counterpart, Sumner's famous Society. Sumner, following the usual procedure, persuaded Lane to withdraw the book pending a court contest and managed to get it banned throughout the country.

This time, however, Sumner ran into a

---

[3] *Current Opinion,* LV (1913), 113–14.
[4] *Dial,* editorial, January 16, 1912, pp. 39–40.

fight. Despite Mencken's correct warnings that anti-German sentiment would be brought into the contest, Dreiser refused to compromise, and Mencken roused a public protest. He failed to get help from Howells, Brander Matthews, and most of the other custodians of culture. Yet he was able to line up a formidable list of libertarians: in England Arnold Bennett, Hugh Walpole, and Wells; in this country Amy Lowell, Robert Frost, Edwin Arlington Robinson, Willa Cather, William Allen White, Knopf, Huebsch, and many others. The book remained substantially suppressed until 1923, but the defenders of intellectual freedom were aroused to battle as never before.

In this battle, and in the whole war that was opening, both sides were serious. To the intellectuals, censors were nasty and cruel old men, inflicting on others their own frustrations, denying to America the possibility of free and joyous self-expression. To some of the conservatives in the prewar years, a strange flood of filth was welling up from mysterious sources. Erotic plays and books, divorce, free love, lascivious dances, birth control were menacing not only American culture but the possibility of moral restraint, the sheet-anchor of any and all civilization.

The *Nation,* balanced and serious as usual, presented a picture of the situation in 1913 which was fairly accurate, given the *Nation's* assumptions. All was not lost, despite:

Tango, eugenics, the slit skirt, sex hygiene, Brieux, white slaves, Richard Strauss, John Masefield, the double standard of morality. . . a conglomerate of things important and unimportant, of age-old problems and momentary fads, which nevertheless have this one thing in common, that they do involve an abandonment of the old proprieties and the old reticences. . . .

One must distinguish, said the *Nation,* between the fluttering tastes of the half-baked intellectuals, attracted by all these things, and the surviving soundness of the great majority. It was still only revolt, not revolution.

JAMES R. McGOVERN (b. 1928) is Professor of
American History at the University of West Florida.
In this article he demonstrates that American women
were already experiencing a new freedom in dress
and behavior before the 1920s. It has usually been
thought that most of what is described here began
only after World War I. By disproving this notion
McGovern enables us to view the changes that came
afterwards in a larger perspective.*

James R. McGovern

Changing Behavior

The Twenties have been alternately
praised or blamed for almost everything
and its opposite; but most historians
hold, whether to praise or to condemn,
that this decade launched the revolution
in manners and morals through which we
are still moving today. This judgment
seems to be part of an even more inclusive
one in American historiography to ex-
ceptionalize the Twenties. No other
decade has invited such titles of historical
caricature as *The Jazz Age, This Was
Normalcy, Fantastic Interim,* or *The
Perils of Prosperity.* Richard Hofstadter's
classic, *The Age of Reform,* subtly
reinforces this view by seeing the Twenties as "Entr'acte," an interim between
two periods of reform, the Progressive
era and the New Deal, which themselves
display discontinuity.

Revisionism, in the form of a develop-
mental interpretation of the relationship
between the Progressive era and the
Twenties, has been gaining strong support in recent years. De-emphasizing the
disruptive impact of World War I, Henry
F. May asked whether the 1920s could be
understood fully "without giving more
attention to the old regime." He declared
that "Immediately prewar America must
be newly explored," especially "its inarticulate assumptions—assumptions in such
areas as morality, politics, class and race
relations, popular art and literature, and

* James R. McGovern, article originally entitled "The American Woman's Pre-World War I Freedom
in Manners and Morals," *Journal of American History,* LV (September, 1968), pp. 315–38. Most footnotes
omitted.

family life." May pursued his inquiry in *The End of American Innocence* and showed that for the purposes of intellectual history, at least, the Twenties were not as significant as the preceding decade. Political historians have been reassessing the relationship of the Progressive era to the Twenties as well. Arthur Link has demonstrated that progressivism survived World War I, and J. Joseph Huthmacher has established continuity between progressivism and the New Deal in the immigrant's steadfast devotion to the ameliorative powers of the government. Together with May's analysis, their writings suggest that the 1920s are much more the result of earlier intrinsic social changes than either the sudden, supposedly traumatic experiences of the war or unique developments in the Twenties. Since this assertion is certain to encounter the formidable claims that the 1920s, at least in manners and morals, amounted to a revolution, its viability can be tested by questioning if the American woman's "emancipation" in manners and morals occurred even earlier than World War I.

Even a casual exploration of the popular literature of the Progressive era reveals that Americans then described and understood themselves to be undergoing significant changes in morals. "Sex o'clock in America" struck in 1913, about the same time as "The Repeal of Reticence." One contemporary writer saw Americans as liberated from the strictures of "Victorianism," now an epithet deserving criticism, and exulted, "Heaven defend us from a return to the prudery of the Victorian regime!"[1] Conditions were such that another commentator asked self-consciously, "Are We Immoral?"[2]

And still another feared that the present "vice not often matched since [the time of] the Protestant Reformation" might invite a return to Puritanism.[3] Yet, historians have not carefully investigated the possibility that the true beginnings of America's "New Freedom" in morals occurred prior to 1920. The most extensive, analytical writing on the subject of changing manners and morals is found in Frederick L. Allen's *Only Yesterday* (1931), William Leuchtenburg's *The Perils of Prosperity* (1958), May's *The End of American Innocence* (1959), and George Mowry's *The Urban Nation* (1965).

Allen and Leuchtenburg apply almost identical sharp-break interpretations, respectively entitling chapters "The Revolution in Manners and Morals" and "The Revolution in Morals." Both catalogue the same types of criteria for judgment. The flapper, as the "new woman" was called, was a creature of the 1920s. She smoked, drank, worked, and played side by side with men. She became preoccupied with sex—shocking and simultaneously unshockable. She danced close, became freer with her favors, kept her own latchkey, wore scantier attire which emphasized her boyish, athletic form, just as she used makeup and bobbed and dyed her hair. She and her comradely beau tried to abolish time and succeeded, at least to the extent that the elders asked to join the revelry. Although there were occasional "advance signals" of "rebellion" before the war, it was not until the 1920s that the code of woman's innocence and ignorance crumbled.

May, who comes closest to an understanding of the moral permissiveness before the 1920s, describes in general

---

[1] H. W. Boynton, "Ideas, Sex, and the Novel," *Dial*, LX (April 13, 1916), 361.

[2] Arthur Pollock, "Are We Immoral?," *Forum*, LI (Jan. 1914), 52. Pollock remarks that "in our literature and in our life to-day sex is paramount."

[3] "Will Puritanism Return?" *Independent*, 77 (March 23, 1914), 397.

terms such phenomena of the Progressive era as the "Dance Craze," birth control, the impact of the movies, and the "white-slave panic." He focuses on the intellectuals, however, and therefore overlooks the depth of these and similar social movements. This causes him to view them as mere "Cracks in the Surface" of an essentially conservative society. He quotes approvingly of the distinction made by the *Nation* "between the fluttering tastes of the half-baked intellectuals, attracted by all these things, and the surviving soundness of the great majority." His treatment also ignores one of the most significant areas of changing manners and morals as they affected the American woman: the decided shift in her sex role and identification in the direction of more masculine norms. Again, *The End of American Innocence* does not convincingly relate these changes to the growth of the cities. Perhaps these limitations explain Mowry's preference for a "sharp-break" interpretation, although he wrote seven years after May.

Mowry, who acknowledges especial indebtedness to Leuchtenburg, is emphatic about the 'startling" changes in manners and morals in the 1920s. He highlights "the new woman of the twenties" whose "modern feminine morality and attitudes toward the institution of marriage date from the twenties." Mowry concedes to the libidos of progressives only the exceptional goings-on in Greenwich Village society.

These hypotheses, excluding May's, hold that the flapper appeared in the postwar period mainly because American women en masse then first enjoyed considerable social and economic freedom. They also emphasize the effect of World War I on morals. By inference, of course, the Progressive era did not provide a suitable matrix. But an investigation of this period establishes that women had become sufficiently active and socially independent to prefigure the "emancipation" of the 1920s.

A significant deterioration of external controls over morality had occurred before 1920. One of the consequences of working and living conditions in the cities, especially as these affected women, was that Americans of the period 1900–1920 had experienced a vast dissolution of moral authority, which formerly had centered in the family and the small community. The traditional "straight and narrow" could not serve the choices and opportunities of city life. As against primary controls and contacts based on face-to-face association where the norms of family, church, and small community, usually reinforcing each other, could be internalized, the city made for a type of "individualization" through its distant, casual, specialized, and transient clusters of secondary associations. The individual came to determine his own behavioral norms.

The "home is in peril" became a fact of sociological literature as early as 1904. One of the most serious signs of its peril was the increasing inability of parents to influence their children in the delicate areas of propriety and morals. The car, already numerous enough to affect dating and premarital patterns, the phone coming to be used for purposes of romantic accommodation, and the variety of partners at the office or the factory, all together assured unparalleled privacy and permissiveness between the sexes.

Individualization of members served to disrupt confidence between generations of the family, if not to threaten parents with the role of anachronistic irrelevance. Dorothy Dix observed in 1913 that there had been "so many changes in the conditions of life and point of view in the last twenty years that the parent of today is absolutely unfitted to decide the problems of life for the young man and woman of to-day. This is particularly the case with women because the whole economic and social position of women has been revolutionized since mother was a girl." Magazine articles lamented "The Passing of the Home Daughter" who preferred the blessed anonymity of the city to "dying of asphyxiation at home!" The same phenomenon helps to explain the popularity in this period of such standardized mothers as Dorothy Dix, Beatrice Fairfax, and Emily Post, each of whom was besieged with queries on the respective rights of mothers and daughters.

Woman's individualization resulted mainly because, whether single or married, gainfully employed or not, she spent more time outside her home. Evidence demonstrates that the so-called job and kitchen revolutions were already in advanced stages by 1910. The great leap forward in women's participation in economic life came between 1900 and 1910; the percentage of women who were employed changed only slightly from 1910 to 1930. A comparison of the percentages of gainfully employed women aged 16 to 44 between 1890 and 1930 shows that they comprised 21.7 percent of Americans employed in 1890, 23.5 percent in 1900, 28.1 percent in 1910, 28.3 percent in 1920, and 29.7 percent in 1930. While occupational activity for women appears to stagnate from 1910 to 1920, in reality a considerable restructuring occurred with women leaving roles as domestics and assuming positions affording more personal independence as clerks and stenographers.

Married women, especially those in the upper and middle classes, enjoyed commensurate opportunities. Experts in household management advised wom-en to rid themselves of the maid and turn to appliances as the "maid of all service." Statistics on money expended on those industries which reduced home labor for the wife suggest that women in middle-income families gained considerable leisure after 1914. This idea is also corroborated from other sources, especially from the tone and content of advertising in popular magazines when they are compared with advertising at the turn of the century. Generally speaking, women depicted in advertising in or about 1900 are well rounded, have gentle, motherly expressions, soft billowy hair, and delicate hands. They are either sitting down or standing motionless; their facial expressions are immobile as are their corseted figures. After 1910, they are depicted as more active figures with more of their activity taking place outside their homes. One woman tells another over the phone: "Yes [,] drive over right away — I'll be ready. My housework! Oh that's all done. How do I do it? I just let electricity do my work nowadays."[4] Vacuum cleaners permitted the housewife to "Push the Button — and Enjoy the Springtime!" Van Camp's "Pork and Beans" promised to save her "100 hours yearly," and Campbell's soups encouraged, "Get some fun out of life," since it was unnecessary to let the "three-meals-a-day problem tie you down to constant drudgery." Wizard Polish, Minute Tapioca and Minute Gelatine also offered the same promise. The advertising image of women became more natural, even nonchalant. A lady entertaining a friend remarks: "I don't have to hurry nowadays. I have a Florence Automatic Oil Stove in my kitchen." It had become "so *very easy*" to wax the floors that well-dressed women could manage them. And they

---

[4] *Collier's*, 56 (Nov. 27, 1915), 4.

enjoyed a round of social activities driving the family car.

It was in this setting that the flapper appeared along with her older married sister who sought to imitate her. No one at the office or in the next block cared much about their morals as long as the one was efficient and the other paid her bills on time. And given the fact that both these women had more leisure and wished "to participate in what men call 'the game of life'" rather than accept "the mere humdrum of household duties," it is little wonder that contemporaries rightly assessed the danger of the situation for traditional morals by 1910.

The ensuing decade was marked by the development of a revolution in manners and morals; its chief embodiment was the flapper who was urban based and came primarily from the middle and upper classes. Young—whether in fact or fancy—assertive, and independent, she experimented with intimate dancing, permissive favors, and casual courtships or affairs. She joined men as comrades, and the differences in behavior of the sexes were narrowed. She became in fact in some degree desexualized. She might ask herself, "Am I Not a Boy? Yes, I Am—Not." Her speech, her interest in thrills and excitement, her dress and hair, her more aggressive sexuality, even perhaps her elaborate beautification, which was a statement of intentions, all point to this. Women, whether single or married, became at once more attractive and freer in their morals and paradoxically less feminine. Indeed, the term sexual revolution as applied to the Progressive era means reversal in the traditional role of women just as it describes a pronounced familiarity of the sexes.

The unmarried woman after 1910 was living in the "Day of the Girl." Dorothy Dix described "the type of girl that the modern young man falls for" in 1915 as a "husky young woman who can play golf all day and dance all night, and drive a motor car, and give first aid to the injured if anybody gets hurt, and who is in no more danger of swooning than he is." Little wonder she was celebrated in song as "A Dangerous Girl"; the lyrics of one of the popular songs for 1916 read, "You dare me, you scare me, and still I like you more each day. But you're the kind that will charm; and then do harm; you've got a dangerous way." The "most popular art print . . . ever issued" by *Puck* depicts a made-up young lady puckering her lips and saying "Take It From Me!" The American girl of 1900 was not described in similar terms. The lovely and gracious Gibson Girl was too idealized to be real. And when young lovers trysted in advertising, they met at Horlick's Malted Milk Bar; he with his guitar, and she with her parasol. Beatrice Fairfax could still reply archaically about the need for "maidenly reserve" to such queries as those on the proprieties of men staring at women on the streets. And the *Wellesley College News* in 1902 reported that students were not permitted to have a Junior Prom because it would be an occasion for meeting "promiscuous men," although the college sanctioned "girl dances."

The girls, however, dispensed with "maidenly reserve." In 1910, Margaret Deland, the novelist, could announce a "Change in the Feminine Ideal."

This young person . . . with surprisingly bad manners—has gone to college, and when she graduates she is going to earn her own living . . . she won't go to church; she has views upon marriage and the birth-rate, and she utters them calmly, while her mother blushes with embarrassment; she occupies herself, passionately, with everything except the things that used to occupy the minds of girls.

Many young women carried their own latchkeys. Meanwhile, as Dorothy Dix noted, it had become "literally true that the average father does not know, by name or sight, the young man who visits his daughter and who takes her out to places of amusement." She was distressed over the widespread use by young people of the car which she called the "devil's wagon." Another writer asked: "Where Is Your Daughter This Afternoon?" "Are you sure that she is not being drawn into the whirling vortex of afternoon 'trots' . . . ?" Polly, Cliff Sterett's remarkable comic-strip, modern girl from *Polly and Her Pals*, washed dishes under the shower and dried them with an electric fan; and while her mother tried hard to domesticate her, Polly wondered, "Gee Whiz! I wish I knew what made my nose shine!"

Since young women were working side by side with men and recreating more freely and intimately with them, it was inevitable that they behave like men. Older people sometimes carped that growing familiarity meant that romance was dead or that "nowadays brides hardly blush, much less faint." And Beatrice Fairfax asked, "Has Sweet Sixteen Vanished?" But some observers were encouraged to note that as girls' ways approximated men's, the sexes were, at least, more comradely. The modern unmarried woman had become a "Diana, Hunting in the Open." Dorothy Dix reported that "nice girls, good girls, girls in good positions in society—frankly take the initiative in furthering an acquaintance with any man who happens to strike their fancy." The new ideal in feminine figure, dress, and hair styles was all semi-masculine. The "1914 Girl" with her "slim hips and boy-carriage" was a "slim, boylike

creature." The "new figure is Amazonian, rather than Miloan. It is boyish rather than womanly. It is strong rather than soft."[5] Her dress styles, meanwhile, de-emphasized both hips and bust while they permitted the large waist. The boyish coiffure began in 1912 when young women began to tuck-under their hair with a ribbon; and by 1913–1914, Newport ladies, actresses like Pauline Frederick, then said to be the prettiest girl in America, and the willowy, popular dancer Irene Castle were wearing short hair. By 1915, the *Ladies Home Journal* featured women with short hair on its covers, and even the pure type of woman who advertised Ivory Soap appeared to be shorn.

The unmarried flapper was a determined pleasure-seeker whom novelist Owen Johnson described collectively as "determined to liberate their lives and claim the same rights of judgment as their brothers." The product of a "feminine revolution startling in the shock of its abruptness," she was living in the city independently of her family. Johnson noted: "She is sure of one life only and that one she passionately desires. She wants to live that life to its fullest. . . . She wants adventure. She wants excitement and mystery. She wants to see, to know, to experience. . . . " She expressed both a "passionate revolt against the commonplace" and a "scorn of conventions." Johnson's heroine in *The Salamander*, Doré Baxter, embodied his views. Her carefree motto is reminiscent of Fitzgerald's flappers of the Twenties: "'How do I know what I'll do to-morrow?'" Her nightly prayer, the modest "'O Lord! give me everything I want!'" Love was her "supreme law of conduct," and she, like the literary flappers of the

---

[5] Boston *American*, June 11, 1916.

Twenties, feared "thirty as a sort of sepulcher, an end of all things!" Johnson believed that all young women in all sections of the country had "a little touch of the Salamander," each alike being impelled by "an impetuous frenzy . . . to sample each new excitement," both the "safe and the dangerous." Girls "seemed determined to have their fling like men," the novelist Gertrude Atherton noted in *Current Opinion*, "and some of the stories [about them] made even my sophisticated hair crackle at the roots. . . ." Beatrice Fairfax deplored the trends, especially the fact that "Making love lightly, boldly and promiscuously seems to be part of our social structure." Young men and women kissed though they did not intend to marry. And kissing was shading into spooning ("'To Spoon' or 'Not to Spoon' Seems to Be the Burning Question with Modern Young America") and even "petting," which was modish among the collegiate set. In fact, excerpts from the diary of a co-ed written before World War I suggest that experimentation was virtually complete within her peer group. She discussed her "adventures" with other college girls. "We were healthy animals and we were demanding our rights to spring's awakening." As for men, she wrote, "I played square with the men. I always told them I was not out to pin them down to marriage, but that this intimacy was pleasant and I wanted it as much as they did. We indulged in sex talk, birth control. . . . We thought too much about it."[6]

One of the most interesting developments in changing sexual behavior which characterized these years was the blurring of age lines between young and middle-aged women in silhouette, dress, and cosmetics. A fashion commentator warned matrons, "This is the day of the figure. . . . The face alone, no matter how pretty, counts for nothing unless the body is as straight and yielding as every young girl's."[7] With only slight variations, the optimum style for women's dress between 1908 and 1918 was a modified sheath, straight up and down and clinging. How different from the styles of the high-busted, broad-hipped mother of the race of 1904 for whom Ella Wheeler Wilcox, the journalist and poet, advised the use of veils because "the slightest approach to masculinity in woman's attire is always unlovely and disappointing."

The sloughing off of numerous undergarments and loosening of others underscored women's quickening activity and increasingly self-reliant morals. Clinging dresses and their "accompanying lack of undergarments" eliminated, according to the president of the New York Cotton Exchange, "at least twelve yards of finished goods for each adult female inhabitant." Corset makers were forced to make adjustments too and use more supple materials. Nevertheless, their sales declined.

The American woman of 1910, in contrast with her sister of 1900, avidly cultivated beauty of face and form. In fact, the first American woman whose photographs and advertising image we can clearly recognize as belonging to our times lived between 1910 and 1920. "Nowadays," the speaker for a woman's club declared in 1916, "only the very poor or the extremely careless are old or ugly. You can go to a beauty shop and choose the kind of beauty you will have."[8] Beautification included the use of powder,

---

[6] Thomas, *Unadjusted Girl*, 95.

[7] Eleanor Chalmers, "Facts and Figures," *Delineator*, LXXXIV (April 1914), 38.

[8] Boston *American*, Dec. 10, 1916.

rouge, lipstick, eyelash and eyebrow stain. Advertising was now manipulating such images for face powder as "Mother tried it and decided to keep it for herself," or "You can have beautiful Eyebrows and Eyelashes. . . . Society women and actresses get them by using Lash-Brow-Ine." Nearly every one of the numerous advertisements for cosmetics promised some variation of "How to Become Beautiful, Fascinating, Attractive."

In her dress as well as her use of cosmetics, the American woman gave evidence that she had abandoned passivity. An unprecedented public display of the female figure characterized the period. Limbs now became legs and more of them showed after 1910, although they were less revealing than the promising hosiery advertisements. Rolled down hose first appeared in 1917. Dresses for opera and restaurant were deeply cut in front and back, and not even the rumor that Mrs. John Jacob Astor has suffered a chest cold as a result of wearing deep decolleté deterred their wearers. As for gowns, "Fashion says—Evening gowns must be sleeveless. . . . afternoon gowns are made with semi-transparent yokes and sleeves."[9] Undoubtedly, this vogue for transparent blouses and dresses caused the editor of the *Unpopular Review* to declare: "At no time and place under Christianity, except the most corrupt periods in France. . . . certainly never before in America, has woman's form been so freely displayed in society and on the street."

In addition to following the example of young women in dress and beautification, middle-aged women, especially those from the middle and upper classes, were espousing their permissive manners and morals. Smoking and, to a lesser extent, drinking in public were becoming fashionable for married women of the upper class and were making headway at other class levels. As early as 1910, a prominent clubwoman stated: "It has become a well-established habit for women to drink cocktails. It is thought the smart thing to do."[10] Even before Gertrude Atherton described in the novel *Black Oxen* the phenomenon of the middle-aged women who sought to be attractive to young men, supposedly typifying the 1920s, it was evident in the play "Years of Discretion." Written by Frederic Hatton and Fanny Locke Hatton, and staged by Belasco, the play was "welcomed cordially both in New York and Chicago" in 1912. It featured a widowed mother forty-eight years of age, who announces, "I intend to look under forty—lots under. I have never attracted men, but I know I can." Again, "I mean to have a wonderful time. To have all sorts and kinds of experience. I intend to love and be loved, to lie and cheat." Dorothy Dix was dismayed over "the interest that women . . . have in what we are pleased to euphoniously term the 'erotic.'" She continued, "I'll bet there are not ten thousand women in the whole United States who couldn't get one hundred in an examination of the life and habits of Evelyn Nesbitt and Harry Thaw. . . ." Married women among the fashionable set held the great parties, at times scandalous ones which made the 1920s seem staid by comparison. They hired the Negro orchestras at Newport and performed and sometimes invented the daring dances. They conscientiously practiced birth control, as did women of other classes. And they initiated divorce proceedings, secure in the knowledge

---

[9] *Cosmopolitan*, LIX (July 1915).

[10] Boston *American*, March 7, 1910.

that many of their best friends had done the same thing.

Perhaps the best insights on the mores and morals of this group are to be found in the writings of the contemporary, realistic novelist, Robert Herrick. Herrick derived his heroines from "the higher income groups, the wealthy, upper middle, and professional classes among which he preferred to move." His heroines resemble literary flappers of the 1920s in their repudiation of childbearing. "It takes a year out of a woman's life, of course, no matter how she is situated," they say, or, "Cows do that." Since their lives were seldom more than a meaningless round of social experiences, relieved principally by romantic literature, many of them either contemplated or consented to infidelity. Thus Margaret Pole confesses to her friend, Conny Woodyard, "'I'd like to lie out on the beach and forget children and servants and husbands, and stop wondering what life is. Yes, I'd like a vacation—in the Windward Islands, with somebody who understood.' 'To wit, a man!' added Conny. 'Yes, a man! But only for the trip.'" They came finally to live for love in a manner that is startlingly reminiscent of some of the famous literary women of the Twenties.

Insights regarding the attitudes of married women from the urban lower middle class can be found in the diary of Ruth Vail Randall, who lived in Chicago from 1911 to the date of her suicide, March 6, 1920. A document of urban sociology, the diary transcends mere personal experience and becomes a commentary on group behavior of the times. Mrs. Randall was reared in a family that owned a grocery store, was graduated from high school in Chicago, and was married at twenty to Norman B. Randall, then twenty-one. She worked after marriage in a department store and later for a brief period as a model. She looked to marriage, especially its romance, as the supreme fulfillment of her life and was bitterly disappointed with her husband. She began to turn to other men whom she met at work or places of recreation, and her husband left her. Fearing that her lover would leave her eventually as well, she killed him and herself.

The diary focuses on those conditions which made the revolution in morals a reality. The young couple lived anonymously in a highly mobile neighborhood where their morals were of their own making. Mrs. Randall did not want children; she aborted their only child. She was also averse to the reserved "womanly" role, which her husband insisted that she assume. She complained, "Why cannot a woman do all man does?" She wished that men and women were more alike in their social roles. She repudiated involvement in her home, resolved to exploit equally every privilege which her husband assumed, drank, flirted, and lived promiscuously. Telephones and cars made her extramarital liaisons possible. Even before her divorce, she found another companion; flouting convention, she wrote, "He and I have entered a marriage pact according to our own ideas." Throughout her diary she entertained enormous, almost magical, expectations of love. She complained that her lovers no more than her husband provided what she craved—tenderness and companionship. Disillusionment with one of them caused her to cry out, "I am miserable. I have the utmost contempt for myself. But the lake is near and soon it will be warm. Oh, God to rest in your arms. To rest—and to have peace."

That America was experiencing a major upheaval in morals during the Progressive era is nowhere better ascertained than in the comprehensive efforts by civic officials and censorial citizens to control them. Disapproval extended not only to such well-known staples as alcohol, divorce, and prostitution, but also to dancing, woman's dress, cabarets, theaters and movies, and birth control. "Mrs. Warren's Profession" was withdrawn from the New York stage in 1905 after a one night performance, the manager of the theater later being charged with offending public decency. When a grand jury in New York condemned the "turkey trot and kindred dances" as "indecent," the judge who accepted the presentment noted that "Rome's downfall was due to the degenerate nature of its dancers, and I only hope that we will not suffer the same result." Public dancing was henceforth to be licensed. Mayor John Fitzgerald personally assisted the morals campaign in Boston by ordering the removal from a store of an objectionable picture which portrayed a "show-girl" with her legs crossed. Meanwhile, the "X-Ray Skirt" was outlawed in Portland, Oregon, and Los Angeles, and the police chief of Louisville, Kentucky, ordered the arrest of a number of women appearing on the streets with slit skirts. Witnessing to a general fear that the spreading knowledge of contraception might bring on sexual license, the federal and several state governments enacted sumptuary legislation. And in two celebrated incidents, the offenders, Van K. Allison (1916) in Boston and Margaret Sanger (1917) in New York, were prosecuted and sent to jail.

Public officials were apprehensive about the sweeping influence of the movies on the masses, "at once their book, their drama, their art. To some it has become society, school, and even church."[11]

They proceeded to set up boards of censorship with powers to review and condemn movies in four states: Pennsylvania (1911), Ohio (1913), Maryland (1916), and Kansas (1917), and in numerous cities beginning with Chicago in 1907. The Pennsylvania board, for example, prohibited pictures which displayed nudity, prolonged passion, women drinking and smoking, and infidelity. It protected Pennsylvanians from such films produced between 1915 and 1918 as "What Every Girl Should Know," "A Factory Magdalene," and "Damaged Goodness."

Such determination proved unavailing, however, even as the regulatory strictures were being applied. According to one critic the "sex drama" using "plain, blunt language" had become "a commonplace" of the theater after 1910 and gave the "tender passion rather the worst for it in recent years." Vice films packed them in every night, especially after the smashing success of "Traffic in Souls," which reportedly grossed $450,000. In Boston the anti-vice campaign itself languished because there was no means of controlling "the kitchenette-apartment section." "In these apartment houses, there are hundreds of women who live as they please and who entertain as they will."[12] Mayor Fitzgerald's "show-girl," evicted from her saucy perch, gained more notoriety when she appeared in a Boston newspaper the following day. Even Anthony Comstock, that indefatigable guardian of public morals, had probably come to look a bit like a comic character living beyond his times.

When Mrs. Sanger was arrested for propagating birth control information in 1917, she confidently stated, "I have nothing to fear. . . . Regardless of the outcome I shall continue my work,

---

[11] *Report of the Pennsylvania Board of Censors,* June 1, 1915 to Dec. 1, 1915 (Harrisburg, 1916), 6.

[12] Boston *American,* July 7, 1917.

supported by thousands of men and women throughout the country." Her assurance was well founded. Three years earlier her supporters had founded a National Birth Control League; and in 1919, this organization opened its first public clinic. But most encouraging for Mrs. Sanger was the impressive testimony that many Americans were now practicing or interested in birth control. When Paul B. Blanchard, pastor of the Maverick Congregational Church in East Boston, protested the arrest of Van K. Allison, he charged, "If the truth were made public and the laws which prevent the spreading of even oral information about birth control were strictly enforced how very few of the married society leaders, judges, doctors, ministers, and businessmen would be outside the prison dock!"

The foregoing demonstrates that a major shift in American manners and morals occurred in the Progressive era, especially after 1910. Changes at this time, though developing out of still earlier conditions, represented such visible departures from the past and were so commonly practiced as to warrant calling them revolutionary. Too often scholars have emphasized the Twenties as the period of significant transition and World War I as a major cause of the phenomenon. Americans of the 1920s, fresh from the innovative wartime atmosphere, undoubtedly quickened and deepened the revolution. Women from smaller cities and towns contested what was familiar terrain to an already seasoned cadre of urban women and a formidable group of defectors. Both in their rhetoric and their practices, apparent even before the war, the earlier group had provided the shibboleths for the 1920s; they first asked, "What are Patterns for?" The revolution in manners and morals was, of course, but an integral part of numerous, contemporary, political and social movements to free the individual by reordering society. Obviously, the Progressive era, more than the 1920s, represents the substantial beginnings of contemporary American civilization.

The revolution in manners and morals, particularly as it affected women, took the twofold form of more permissive sexuality and diminished femininity. Women from the upper classes participated earlier, as is evidenced by their introductory exhibition of fashions, hair styles, dances, cosmetics, smoking, and drinking. Realistic novels concerned with marriage suggest that they entertained ideas of promiscuity and even infidelity before women of the lower classes. Yet the cardinal condition of change was not sophistication but urban living and the freedom it conferred. As technology and economic progress narrowed the gap between the classes, middle-class women and even those below were free to do many of the same things almost at the same time. Above all, the revolution in manners and morals after 1910 demonstrates that sexual freedom and the twentieth century American city go together.

WILLIAM E. LEUCHTENBURG (b. 1922) is Professor
of American History at Columbia University. In this
lively and concise essay he portrays the new morality
and the new woman as they seemed at birth. The views
represented are still widely shared by historians.*

William E. Leuchtenburg

The Revolution in Morals

The disintegration of traditional American values—so sharply recorded by novelists and artists—was reflected in a change in manners and morals that shook American society to its depths. The growing secularization of the country greatly weakened religious sanctions. People lost their fear of Hell and at the same time had less interest in Heaven; they made more demands for material fulfillment on Earth. The "status revolution" of the turn of the century undercut the authority of the men who had set America's moral standards: the professional classes, especially ministers, lawyers, and teachers; the rural gentry; the farmers; the urban patricians. The new urban minorities and *arriviste* businessmen were frequent-

ly not equipped—not even aware of the need either to support old standards or to create new ones. Most important, the authority of the family, gradually eroded over several centuries, had been sharply lessened by the rise of the city. "Never in recent generations," wrote Freda Kirchwey, "have human beings so floundered about outside the ropes of social and religious sanctions."

When Nora, the feminist heroine of *A Doll's House* (1879) by the Norwegian playwright Henrik Ibsen, walked out into the night, she launched against male-dominated society a rebellion that has not ended yet. The "new woman" revolted against masculine possessiveness, against "over-evaluation" of wo-

*From William E. Leuchtenburg, *The Perils Of Prosperity 1914–32* (Chicago: The University of Chicago Press, 1958), Ch. 9. © 1958 by The University of Chicago. Used by permission of the University of Chicago and William E. Leuchtenburg.

men "as love objects," against being treated, at worst, as a species of property. The new woman wanted the same freedom of movement that men had and the same economic and political rights. By the end of the 1920s she had come a long way. Before the war, a lady did not set foot in a saloon; after the war, she entered a speakeasy as thoughtlessly as she would go into a railroad station. In 1904, a woman was arrested for smoking on Fifth Avenue; in 1929, railroads dropped their regulation against women smoking in dining cars. In the business and political worlds, women competed with men; in marriage, they moved toward a contractual role. Once ignorant of financial matters, they moved rapidly toward the point where they would be the chief property-holders of the country. Sexual independence was merely the most sensational aspect of the generally altered status of women.

In 1870, there were only a few women secretaries in the entire country; by the time of World War I, two million women worked in business offices, typing the letters and keeping the records of corporations and counting-houses in every city in the nation. During the war, when mobilization created a shortage of labor, women moved into jobs they had never held before. They made grenades, ran elevators, polished locomotives, collected streetcar fares, and even drilled with rifles. In the years after the war, women flew airplanes, trapped beaver, drove taxis, ran telegraph lines, worked as deep-sea divers and steeplejacks, and hunted tigers in the jungle; women stevedores heaved cargoes on the waterfront, while other women conducted orchestras, ran baseball teams, and drilled oil wells. By 1930, more than ten million women held jobs. Nothing

did more to emancipate them. Single women moved into their own apartments, and wives, who now frequently took jobs, gained the freedom of movement and choice that went along with leaving home.

After nearly a century of agitation, women won the suffrage in 1920 with the adoption of the Nineteenth Amendment. The American suffragettes modeled themselves on their British counterparts, who blew up bridges, hurled bombs, and burned churches, activities previously regarded as the exclusive privilege of Irish rebels. Using less violent methods, American women had greater success, and the adoption of the suffrage amendment climaxed a long debate in which suffragettes argued that the advent of the women's vote would initiate a new era of universal peace and benevolence, while their enemies forecast a disintegration of American society. (The chief result of women's suffrage, Mencken predicted, would be that adultery would replace boozing as the favorite pastime of politicians.)

As it turned out, women's suffrage had few consequences, good or evil. Millions of women voted (although never in the same proportion as men), women were elected to public office (several gained seats in Congress by the end of the 1920s), but the new electorate caused scarcely a ripple in American political life. Women like Jane Addams made great contributions, but it would be difficult to demonstrate that they accomplished any more after they had the vote than before. It was widely believed, although never proved, that women cast a "dry" vote for Hoover in 1928 and that women were likely to be more moved than men to cast a "moral-issue" vote. Otherwise, the earth spun around much as it had before.

The extreme feminists argued that women were equal to men, and even more so. "Call on God, my dear," Mrs. Belmont is alleged to have told a despondent young suffragette. "She will help you." Female chauvinists wanted not merely sexual equality but, insofar as possible, to dispense with sexuality altogether, because they conceived of sexual intercourse as essentially humiliating to women. "Man is the only animal using this function out of season," protested Charlotte Perkins Gilman. "Excessive indulgence in sex-waste has imperiled the life of the race." Chanting slogans like "Come out of the kitchen" and "Never darn a sock," feminist leaders rebelled against the age-old household roles of women; before long, even a woman contented with her familiar role felt called on to apologize that she was "just a housewife."

In Dorothy Canfield Fisher's *The Home-Maker* (1924), the process is taken to its logical conclusion: a woman who has been a failure as a mother succeeds in business while her husband, a failure in business, stays at home and makes a success of raising children. The literature of the time reflects the growing male sense of alarm, notably in D. H. Lawrence's morbid fear that he would be absorbed and devoured by woman but even more in a new American character represented by the destructive Nina Leeds of O'Neill's *Strange Interlude* (1928), the husband-exploiting title figure of George Kelly's *Craig's Wife* (1926), and the possessive "son-devouring tigress" of Sidney Howard's *The Silver Cord* (1927).

The new freedom for women greatly increased the instability of the family. By the turn of the century, women were demanding more of marriage than they ever had before and were increasingly unwilling to continue alliances in which they were miserable. For at least a century, the family had been losing many of its original social and economic functions; the state, the factory, the school, and even mass amusements robbed the family of functions it once had. The more that social usefulness was taken away from the family, the more marriage came to depend on the personalities of the individuals involved, and, since many Americans of both sexes entered marriage with unreasonable expectations, this proved a slender reed. In 1914, the number of divorces reached 100,000 for the first time; in 1929, over 205,000 couples were divorced in a single year. The increase in divorce probably meant less an increase in marital unhappiness than a refusal to go on with marriages which would earlier have been tolerated.

As the family lost its other social functions, the chief test of a good family became how well it developed the personalities of the children, and parents, distrustful both of their own instincts and of tribal lore, eagerly sought out expert advice to avoid the opprobrium of having raised unhappy children. Dr. John B. Watson published the first edition of *Behaviorism* in 1914, but it was not until its third edition in 1925 that behaviorism—the idea that man was nothing but a machine responding to stimuli—took the country by storm. Since man was only a machine, environment alone was significant in determining both man's character and the nature of his society. "Give me a dozen healthy infants, well-formed, and my own specified world to bring them up in," declared Watson, "and I'll guarantee to take any one at random and train him to become any specialist I might select—doctor, lawyer, artist, merchant-chief, and yes, even beggarman and thief, regardless of his talents, tendencies, abilities, vocations and race of his ancestor." Watson's theories had the greatest impact on childrearing; the Department of Labor incorporated behaviorist assumptions in its pamphlet *Infant and Child Care,* which, with emphasis on rigid scheduling of a baby's activities, became the government's leading best seller. Watson predicted that the time would come when it would be just as bad manners to show affection to one's mother or father as to come to the table with dirty hands. To inculcate the proper attitudes at an early age, Watson warned parents, "Never hug and kiss them, never let them sit in your lap."

Great as Watson's influence was, it could not hold a candle to that of Sigmund Freud. Before the war, Freud's name was known, outside of medical circles, only to a coterie of intellectuals. He had been referred to in the United States as early as 1895 by Dr. Robert Edes, but, a decade later, only a few well-informed medical men knew his name. By 1908, Dr. A. A. Brill, who had studied at Jung's Clinic of Psychiatry in Zurich, was won to Freudian theory and undertook the major task of translating Freud's work. In 1909, when Freud journeyed to the United States to give a series of lectures at Clark University, he was amazed that "even in prudish America" his work was so well known. The following year, Brill published the first of his translations of Freud, *Three Contributions to a Theory of Sex* (previously available only in the German *Drei Adhandlungen zur Sexual-Theorie*), and in 1913, Brill, at the invitation of the precocious Walter Lippmann, explained Freud to a group of American intellectuals gathered at Mabel Dodge's salon.

With startling speed Freudian doctrine was acknowledged by a number of American intellectuals; in 1915 Lippmann and Max Eastman wrote perceptive articles on him, and his work, along with that of Nietzsche and Bergson, had strongly influenced Lippmann's *A Preface to Politics* (1914). Freud's sexual theories, particularly his contention that neurotic symptoms could be traced to sexual disturbances, were not popularly disseminated until after the war. But they were well enough known to New York social workers that, despite hostility and even revulsion at his blunt descriptions of infant sexuality, Brill was able to lecture on "Masturbation" to the ladies of the Child Study Association.

At the same time, Freudian theories made headway against vehement opposition in American medical circles. By 1916 there were some five hundred psychoanalysts, or people who called themselves that, in New York City. American participation in the war made the whole country psychology-conscious, if not Freud-conscious; more than one hundred psychologists served on the Surgeon-General's staff, and there was wide discussion of wartime medical phenomena like "shell shock." Even more important in popularizing psychology were the Army "intelligence" tests and the debates they aroused; during the war, hundreds of thousands of soldiers were asked to cross out the "g" in "tiger."

In the years after the war, psychology became a national mania. Books appeared on the *Psychology of Golf,* the *Psychology of the Poet Shelley,* and the *Psychology of Selling Life Insurance.* People talked knowingly of "libido," "defense mechanism," and "fixation," confused the subconscious with the unconscious, repression with suppression, and dealt with the tortuously difficult theories of Freud and of psychoanalysis as though they were simple ideas readily grasped after a few moments' explanation. One article explained solemnly that the immense popularity of the song "Yes, We Have No Bananas" was the result of a national inferiority complex. Psychiatrist Karl Menninger found himself badgered at parties to perform analyses of the personalities of guests as though he were a fortune teller. "When I refuse," he explained, "my questioners often show me how the thing is done." Neophytes were able to read books like *Psychoanalysis by Mail* and *Psychoanalysis Self-Applied,* while the Sears, Roebuck catalogue offered *Ten Thousand Dreams Interpreted* and *Sex Problems Solved.* Like the automobile, Freud was brought within the reach of everyone.

Freud's popularity had an inevitable effect on the "revolution in morals." It was assumed that he was arguing that unless you freely expressed your libido and gave outlet to your sex energy, you would damage your health; by the distortion of his work, a scientific imprimatur was given to self-indulgence. By a similar but more understandable misinterpretation, it was believed that Freud was denying the reality of love; his name was invoked in support of the dehumanization of sex. "I'm hipped on Freud and all that," observed a Scott Fitzgerald heroine, "but it's rotten that every bit of *real* love in the world is ninety-nine percent passion and one little soupçon of jealousy."

What only the initiate understood was that although Freud did emphasize the strong power of unconscious motivation, psychiatry was aimed not at stressing the irrational or at licensing indulgence but at making it possible for man to use his rational powers to control unconscious forces. Freud taught that the most "irrational" act had meaning. Psychiatrists used Freud's theories to enable men to

control their emotions through a clearer understanding of their irrational impulses. The vast popularity of Freud in America, which was to move the center of psychiatry from Vienna to Park Avenue, alarmed many psychoanalysts. They realized that the popularity had been achieved less through an understanding of Freud than through a belief that he shared the American conviction that every man had the right not merely to pursue happiness but to possess it. This distortion had a number of unfortunate results, not least of which was the disappointment patients experienced when they came to realize that progress could be made only when self-indulgent fantasies were surrendered; but its ultimate effect was good. In Europe, psychiatry followed a course of near-fatalism in treating mental illness; in the more optimistic and more expectant American environment, psychiatry made greater gains and received far greater public support.

Freudian theories had a great impact on American writers, in part because they suggested new techniques for the exploration of human motivation, in part because they gave post-war intellectuals an invaluable weapon against the older standards. In some works the use of Freud was explicit; in others, as in the novels of Sherwood Anderson, where the influence of Freud seems obvious, there was apparently no conscious use of Freud at all. Eugene O'Neill turned to Freudian themes in his ambitious *Strange Interlude* (1928) as well as in his *Desire Under the Elms* (1924) and *Mourning Becomes Electra* (1931). Freud's greatest impact on the form of the novel was in the "stream-of-consciousness" technique, although its most important exponent, the Irish novelist James Joyce, was more directly influenced by

Jung than by Freud. Stream of consciousness was employed in America most notably in William Faulkner's *The Sound and the Fury* (1929) and in the works of the novelist and poet Conrad Aiken. "I decided very early," Aiken recalled, "that Freud, and his co-workers and rivals and followers, were making the most important contribution of the century to the understanding of man and his consciousness; accordingly I made it my business to learn as much from them as I could."

Freud's theories also opened up a new world to biographers anxious to understand the inner life of their subjects, but most of his effect on biography ran from the unfortunate to the disastrous. His own *Leonardo da Vinci* (1910), which should have served as a warning to biographers, became instead a model. In this essay Freud attempted with doubtful success to reconstruct Da Vinci's life and to interpret his works from a single fantasy that Da Vinci remembered. With similar fragmentary evidence, psychoanalytically oriented biographers tried to add a new dimension to their work; some of these ventures were serious, others were little more than vendettas on heroes of the past. Emerson and Thoreau, Ludwig Lewisohn wrote, were "chilled under-sexed valetudinarians." Even when new information or interpretations were established, it was not always clear what use could be made of them. "The superstition persisted," wrote Alfred Kazin, "that to have proved one's subject impotent was to have made a critical statement."

In the attempt to work out a new standard of relations between men and women, Americans in the 1920s became obsessed with the subject of sex. Some novelists wrote of little else, in particular James Branch Cabell, whose *Jurgen*

(1919), actually a curiously unerotic novel despite its absorption with the subject, was praised for its "phallic candour." Radio singers crooned songs like "Hot Lips," "Baby Face," "I Need Lovin'," and "Burning Kisses." Magazines like *Paris Nights, Flapper Experiences,* and *Snappy Stories* covered newsstands. The newspaperman Frank Kent returned from a tour of the country in 1925 with the conviction that "between the magazines and the movies a lot of these little towns seem literally saturated with sex." Advertising, once pristine, began the transition which, as one writer remarked, was to transmute soap from a cleansing agent to an aphrodisiac and to suggest "that every woman buying a pair of stockings is aiming for an assignation, or at the very least for a rescue via a fire-ladder."

Absorption with sex was the life's blood of the newspaper tabloid. Developed by Lord Northcliffe in England, the tabloid first appeared in America with the founding of the New York *Daily News* in 1919. As a picture newspaper like the *Sketch* and the *Mirror* in England, the *News* caught on immediately; within five years it had the largest circulation of any newspaper in New York. Hearst followed with the *New York Daily Mirror,* a slavish imitation of the *News,* and in 1924 Bernarr MacFadden demonstrated how far salacious sensationalism could be carried with the *New York Evening Graphic.* The New York tabloids soon had their imitators in other cities. Although the tabloids won millions of readers, they did not cut into the circulation of the established newspapers; they found a new, semiliterate market.

Not even the tabloids exploited sex with the zeal of Hollywood; it was the movies which created the American love goddess. When the "vamp," Theda Bara, appeared in *The Blue Flame* in 1920, crowds mobbed theaters in eastern cities to get in. Movie producers found that films like *The Sheik* drew large audiences, while *Sentimental Tommy* or epics like *America* played to empty houses. When it was apparent that sex was infinitely more profitable than the prewar sentimental-patriotic fustian, the country got a steady diet of movies like *Up in Mabel's Room,* *Her Purchase Price,* and *A Shocking Night.* (Cecil B. De Mille changed the title of Sir James Barrie's *The Admirable Crichton* into *Male and Female.*) Clara Bow was featured as the "It" girl, and no one had to be told what "it" was. The only ones in Hollywood with "it," explained the novelist Elinor Glyn, were "Rex, the wild stallion, actor Tony Moreno, the Ambassador Hotel doorman and Clara Bow." Movie ads promised kisses "where heart, and soul, and sense in concert move, and the blood is lava, and the pulse a blaze."

Threatened by censorship bills in thirty-six states, the industry made a gesture toward reforming itself. Following the model of organized baseball, which had made Judge Kenesaw Mountain Landis its "czar" after the Chicago Black Sox scandal of 1919, the movie industry hired Harding's Postmaster-General, Will Hays, to be the "Judge Landis of the movies." All the Hays Office succeeded in doing in the 1920s was to add hypocrisy to sex by insisting on false moralizations and the "moral" ending. Movie ads continued to entice patrons with "brilliant men, beautiful jazz babies, champagne baths, midnight revels, petting parties in the purple dawn, all ending in one terrific smashing climax that makes you gasp."

Taboos about sex discussion were lifted; women talked freely about inhibitions and "sex starvation." Speech became bolder, and men and women told one another off-color stories that a short while before would have been reserved for the Pullman smoker. Novelists and playwrights spoke with a new bluntness; in Hemingway's *The Sun Also Rises* (1926), the word "bitch" recurs frequently. The woman who once was shocked by everything now prided herself, observed a writer in *Harper's,* on the fact that nothing at all shocked her; "immunity to the sensation of 'recoil with painful astonishment' is the mark of our civilization."

Parental control of sex was greatly lessened; the chaperone vanished at dances, and there was no room for a duenna in the rumble seat of an automobile. The bachelor girl had her own latchkey. Girls petted, and when they did not pet, they necked, and no one was certain of the exact difference; Lloyd Morris observed: "The word 'neck' ceased to be a noun; abruptly became a verb; immediately lost all anatomical precision." At one conference in the Midwest, eight hundred college girls met to discuss petting, to deal with searching questions like What do nice girls do? and How far should you go? "Whether or not they pet," said one writer, "they hesitate to have anyone believe that they do not." The consensus of the delegates was: "Learn temperance in petting, not abstinence."

Victorian dance forms like the waltz yielded to the fast-stepping Charleston, the Black Bottom, or slow fox trots in which, to the syncopated rhythms of the jazz band, there was a "maximum of motion in the minimum of space." Jazz made its way northward from the bordellos of New Orleans to the dance halls of Chicago during these years, crossed the ocean to Paris (where it was instantly taken up as a uniquely American contribution to music), and created its own folk heroes in the lyrical Bix Beiderbecke and the dynamic Louis Armstrong who, legend has it, once played two hundred different choruses of "Sweet Sue." The tango and the fox trot hit the country before the war, but it was not until the 1920s that the more voluptuous and the more frenetic dance crazes swept the nation. Moralists like Bishop Cannon protested that the new dances brought "the bodies of men and women in unusual relations to each other"; but by the end of the period the fox trot was as popular and the saxophones wailed as loudly at the high-school dances of the Bishop's Methodist parishioners as in the dance halls of New York and Los Angeles.

What did it all add up to? Lord Birkenhead, the British Lord High Chancellor, observed in 1928: "The proportion of frail to virtuous women is probably constant throughout the ages in any civilization." Perhaps, but the meager evidence suggests otherwise. There appears to have been an increase in promiscuity, especially in sexual experience before marriage for middle-class women; there was probably an increase in extramarital experience as well. With effective contraceptive techniques widely used, the fear of pregnancy was greatly lessened. ("The veriest schoolgirl today knows as much as the midwife of 1885," wrote Mencken.) At the same time, quite possibly as a consequence, a great many brothels lost their customers and had to close their doors, while itinerant workers in the same field disappeared from the sidewalks. The degree of sexual experimentation in the 1920s has certainly been exaggerated, but there is a good deal to bear out Alexander Pope's aphorism that "every woman is at heart a rake."

Not only the American woman but the American girl was reputed to be freer with her sexual favors than she had ever been

before, although serious periodicals published learned debates over whether this was fact or fiction. The flapper had as many defenders as accusers on this score, but no one doubted that every campus had its Jezebels. Smith College girls in New York, noted Malcolm Cowley, modeled themselves on Hemingway's Lady Brett. Certainly, girls were less reticent than they had been before the war. "One hears it said," lamented a Southern Baptist periodical, "that the girls are actually tempting the boys more than the boys do the girls, by their dress and conversation." They dressed more freely; they wore bathing suits which revealed more than had ever been revealed before. At dances, corsets were checked in cloakrooms; then even this pretense was abandoned. Above all, they were out for a good time. "None of the Victorian mothers," wrote F. Scott Fitzgerald in *This Side of Paradise*, "had any idea how casually their daughters were accustomed to be kissed."

Although Fitzgerald reported that the ideal flapper was "lovely and expensive and about nineteen," the flapper appeared bent on playing down her femininity and emphasizing her boyishness. She used the most ingenious devices to conceal the fact that she had breasts. Even the nudes at the Folies Bergères were flatchested and were picked for that reason, and in England, women wore the "Eton crop" and bound their chests with wide strips of ribbon to achieve a "boyish bust." The flapper wore dresses that suggested she had no hips at all; her waistline moved steadily southward. As one writer recalled, "Women not only lost their waists; they sat on them." She dieted recklessly in an effort to remove unwanted protuberances. Girls, noted Dr. Charles F. Pabst, were attempting to become "pathologically thin." "A strikingly sad example of improper dieting," he said, "was the case of a shapely motion-picture actress, who became a nervous wreck and blasted her career by restricting herself to tomatoes, spinach and orange juice." The flapper bobbed her hair and dyed it raven black. She concealed everything feminine but her matchstick legs. In 1919 her skirt was six inches above the ground; by 1927 it had edged about to her knees. The well-accoutered flapper wore a tight felt hat, two strings of beads, bangles on her wrists, flesh-colored stockings rolled below the knees, and unbuckled galoshes. Ironically, the more she adopted mannish styles, the more she painted her face, daubing her cheeks with two circles of rouge and her lips with "kissproof" lipstick; cosmetics became the chief way of distinguishing feminine members of the race.

The vogue of the flapper was only the most obvious instance of the new American cult of youth. "It is the glory of the present age that in it one can be young," Randolph Bourne wrote in 1913. In every age, youth has a sense of a separate destiny, of experiencing what no one has ever experienced before, but it may be doubted that there was ever a time in American history when youth had such a special sense of importance as in the years after World War I. There was a break between generations like a geological fault; young men who had fought in the trenches felt that they knew a reality their elders could not even imagine. Young girls no longer consciously modeled themselves on their mothers, whose experience seemed unusable in the 1920s.

Instead of youth modeling itself on age, age imitated youth. Scott Fitzgerald, looking back on the years of which he was the chief chronicler, recalled: "May one offer in exhibit the year 1922! That was the peak of the younger generation, for though the Jazz Age continued, it became less and less an affair of youth. The sequel was a children's party taken over by elders." "Oh, yes, we are collegiate" was the theme song of a generation yearning for the irresponsible, idealized days of youth. Everyone wanted to be young. Mrs. Gertrude Atherton's *Black Oxen* (1923) described how grandmothers might be rejuvenated through a glandular operation and once more stir up young men. It was the young girl who started the flapper ideal; it was her mother who kept it going.

Americans in the 1920s, at least on the surface, were less sinridden and more self-indulgent than they had ever been before. They broke the Sabbath apparently without compunction, missing the morning sermon to play golf, driving into the country in the afternoon instead of sitting stiffly in the parlor. The mood of the country was hedonistic; Omar Khayyam's quatrains took the colleges by storm. The ideal of hedonism was living for the moment, and if one can isolate a single spirit which permeated every segment of society in the postwar years, it was the obliteration of time.

Abandoning the notion of saving income or goods or capital over time, the country insisted on immediate consumption, a demand which became institutionalized in the installment plan. The President's Research Committee on Social Trends noted "the new attitude towards hardship as a thing to be avoided by living in the here and now, utilizing installment credit and other devices to telescope the future into the present." Songs became obsolescent almost as soon as they appeared, and people prided themselves not on remembering the old songs but on knowing the latest. The imitation of youth by age was an effort to telescope the years, while youth itself tried to escape the inexorability of time. One of the younger generation, replying to its critics, observed: "The trouble with them is that they can't seem to realize that we are busy, that what pleasure we snatch must be incidental and feverishly hurried. We have to make the most of our time. . . . We must gather rose-buds while we may."

In the magazine *Secession,* a group of intellectuals, including Hart Crane, Kay Boyle, and Elliot Paul, signed a "Proclamation" declaring "Time is a tyranny to be abolished." Gertrude Stein's concept of a "continuous present" effaced not merely history and tradition but any sense of "time." "The future," she declared, "is not important any more." In Italy, the Futurists had cast out Petrarch and Dante and rejected harmony and sentiment; their present-mindedness had a direct impact on Ezra Pound, who found their chief spokesman, Marinetti, "thoroughly simpatico." The characters in the novels of the day, particularly those of Scott Fitzgerald, lived only for the moment, while Edna St. Vincent Millay penned the theme of the generation in "My candle burns at both ends." The spirit of hedonism of the decade, wrote Edmund Wilson, was "letting oneself be carried along by the mad hilarity and heartbreak of jazz, living only for the excitement of the evening."

The obliteration of time carried with it a conscious assault on the authority of history. The Dada movement, which developed in the war years in Zurich, adopted as its motto: "Je ne veux même pas savoir s'il y a eu des hommes avant moi" ("I do not wish even to know whether there have been men before me"). More remarkably, the very men who were the spokesmen for history and tradition led the onslaught; in this, Henry Ford and Charles Beard were one. Ford's interest in history was actually an anti-history.

He took cottages in which Noah Webster and Patrick Henry had once lived and moved them to Dearborn, Michigan, where they had no meaning. He sentimentalized and pillaged the past, but he had no respect for it. "History is more or less the bunk," he said. "We want to live in the present, and the only history that is worth a tinker's dam is the history we make today." As early as 1907, the historians Charles Beard and James Harvey Robinson had deliberately attempted to subordinate the past to the present with the aim of enabling the reader "to catch up with his own times; . . . to know what was the attitude of Leo XIII toward the Social Democrats even if he has forgotten that of Innocent III toward the Albigenses." Beard's emphasis on current history had its counterpart in Veblen's dislike for dead languages, Holmes's skepticism about the value of learning as a guide in jurisprudence, and Dewey's emphasis on the functional in education.

The revolution in morals routed the worst of Victorian sentimentality and false modesty. It mitigated the harsh moral judgments of rural Protestantism, and it all but wiped out the awful combination of sanctimoniousness and lewdness which enabled Anthony Comstock to defame Bernard Shaw as "this Irish smut-dealer" and which allowed Teddy Roosevelt, with unconscious humor, to denounce the Mexican bandit Villa as a "murderer and a bigamist." It greatly extended the range of choice; "the conduct of life," wrote Joseph Wood Krutch, had been made "more thrillingly difficult." Yet, at the same time, it raised baffling problems of the relations between husband and wife, parent and child, and, in itself, provided no ready guides to conduct. The hedonism of the period was less a solution than a pathological symptom of what Walter Lippmann called a "vast dissolution of ancient habits," and it rarely proved as satisfying as people hoped. "Sons and daughters of the puritans, the artists and writers and utopians who flocked to Greenwich Village to find a frank and free life for the emotions and senses, felt at their backs the icy breath of the monster they were escaping," wrote Joseph Freeman. "Because they could not abandon themselves to pleasure without a sense of guilt, they exaggerated the importance of pleasure, idealized it and even sanctified it."

KENNETH A. YELLIS (b. 1943) is a graduate student in history at the University of Rochester. This essay is especially useful for the connections it draws between changing feminine models and the merchandisers who cater to them. Has the selling of feminine images changed greatly since the 1920s? Are the relations between consumers and producers more complex now because of the mass media and other new developments? If one were to examine other aspects of consumer capitalism would they be much like the fashion world?"*

Kenneth A. Yellis

The Flapper

The flapper wore her hair short in a "Ponjola" bob, a style initiated in this country by the dancer Irene Castle in the mid-1910s, but still considered radical at the end of the war. For hundreds of years women's hair—whether worn up or down, natural or wigged, powdered or oiled—had been long. The flapper covered her head and forehead with a cloche-style hat, tweezed her eyebrows, and used a whole range of other cosmetic devices, including trying to make her mouth look small and puckered, "bee-stung" like Clara Bow's. Her dresses were tight, straight, short and rather plain, with a very low waist, usually about the hips, low necks for evening wear, and short sleeves, or none at all.

She wore nude-colored silk or rayon stockings which she often rolled below the knee, or omitted altogether in hot weather, and high-heeled cut-out slippers or pumps. Underneath her outergarments she wore as little as possible. The corset was replaced by a girdle or nothing at all, and a brassière-like garment was worn to minimize the breasts.

The term "flapper" originated in England as a description of girls of the awkward age, the mid-teens. The awkwardness was meant literally, and a girl who flapped had not yet reached mature, dignified womanhood. The flapper "was supposed to need a certain type of clothing—long, straight lines to cover her awkwardness—and the stores advertised these gowns as 'flapper-dresses.'"[1] It was in postwar America that these gawky, boyish flappers became the aesthetic ideal.

The major component of this ideal was a displacement of exposure and emphasis from the trunk to the limbs, "in order that the long lines and graceful contours of the arm [and leg] may be fully appreciated." The aesthetic ideal was, in a word, youth:

Long slender limbs and an undeveloped torso are typical of immaturity, and, if modesty has departed from the legs, it has now moved upwards to the body, where any display of the (formerly so much admired) characteristics of the fuller figure is discountenanced. The bosom must be small and virginal, and maturity . . . is concealed as long as possible.[2]

This abandonment of the traditional female aesthetic paralleled the rejection by many women of the passive sexual, social and economic role from which it had derived its force and relevance.

All the previous kinds of clothing for women in the west were appropriate for the kind of woman who existed at that time, but there was no precedent for dressing the woman who seemed to be emerging in the 1920s. But even without such a precedent, a proper dress for her needs was found. It was much more light and comfortable than women's apparel had been for a long time, there were many fewer garments and the fabrics were less stiff and rigid, offering great flexibility and freedom of movement. A greater variety of fabrics, colors, types of clothing, and designs were available than ever before. Bones and stays and long skirts seemed to have gone forever.

---

[1] Elizabeth Sage, *A Study of Costume* (New York, 1926), p. 216.

[2] John C. Flügel, *The Psychology of Clothes* (London, 1930), p. 202.

Economy, simplicity and durability were the watchwords. Inexpensive clothing that stayed out of one's way and could be cared for easily was increasingly in demand and manufacturers made it available. Basic colors became important because of the economy and simple elegance they offered; black and beige were the most popular in the 1920s. Infinite permutations of a limited wardrobe were made possible by a multitude of inexpensive and attractive accessories such as stockings, shoes, gloves, handbags and costume jewelry. As a number of observers remarked, even the poorest women had it in their power to dress comfortably and attractively for an active life with minimal cost and care.

The Lynds observed that in Middletown, at least, furnace-heated houses and enclosed automobiles seemed to have obviated much of the function of clothing as physical protection. Moreover, it seemed to them that its moral function, at least for women, had been modified considerably. They cited the Middletown high-school boy who confidently remarked that his generation's most important contribution to civilization was the one-piece bathing suit for women. Middletown's women and girls had shortened their skirts from the ground to the knee and their "lower limbs have been emphasized by sheer silk stockings; more of the arms and neck are habitually exposed; while the increasing abandonment of petticoats and corsets reveals more of the natural contours of the body." A high-school girl in Middletown typically wore to school only a brassière, knickers (an undergarment), knee-length dress, low shoes and silk stockings. Though some in Middletown felt that these developments were "a violation of morals and good taste," a revue staged in the high-school auditorium featured locally prominent recent high-school alumnae dancing with backs bare to the waist and bare thighs. Moreover, the contrast between the amount of clothing ordinarily worn by men and by women in the 1920s is suggestive:

Men still cover the body modestly from chin to soles, but women are (or were) rolling up from below, down from above, and in from the sides. In summer, men wear four times as much clothes by weight as women.[3]

A certain amount of qualification is necessary here. Obviously not every American woman was a flapper, nor was the flapper herself uniform throughout the decade. Nevertheless, what was true of the flapper was true of fashionable women fairly generally, and somewhat less true of a whole range of women not strictly fashionable, but not totally out of it either. Perusal of the Sears, Roebuck catalogues for the decade is very suggestive in this respect. These catalogues were, presumably, important to women in areas and situations in which being strictly fashionable was not vital for their careers or social acceptance, such as women on farms or in towns out of the reach of the large urban department stores. But the styles in these catalogues, not only in dresses but in hats, coats, shoes, lingerie, cosmetics and accessories, were no more than three months behind what was readily available in New York department stores.

Moreover, the language of the descriptions of the items in the catalogue echoed *Vogue,* seeking to sell the garments by virtue of their fashionableness, their exactness in duplicating what was in New York shop windows and on Parisian manikins. Even the designs that Sears characterized as conservative were quite modish. And most importantly, the prices ranged from quite low to moderate, making it possible for most of the women who got the Sears catalogue to be very well dressed for a modest outlay.

Thus, the flapper was an ideal to be emulated, which it was possible for many women to do quite easily, and which they seem to have done. But what was the relation of this ideal to reality? Why did women seek to emphasize freedom and play down femininity in their dress? What made it possible and neccessary for them to do so? One of the most frequent defenses women made of the current modes was their convenience. But convenience for what?

Increasingly in the postwar years, and as part of a long-term economic trend, women, whether married or single, were working to support themselves or to supplement their families' incomes. Moreover, they were penetrating all kinds of businesses and professions previously barely touched by ladylike hands. The economic independence, greater opportunity and ability to find personal satisfaction outside of the home life in which women had traditionally found fulfillment were both consequences and reinforcing causes of the social and sexual independence women were now beginning to exercise and which expressed itself in dress.

The ideal woman now, for those who did not work as well as for those who did, was self-sufficient, intelligent, capable and active. She possessed skills and had acquired needs unknown to her mother. The influx of well-educated single and married middle-class women into the professions, public service and business resulted in the creation of a new class of women who constituted a growing and lucrative market, especially for clothes. This market could easily be tapped if the right clothes were found, and they were. These working women

---

[3] Stuart Chase, *Prosperity—Fact or Myth?* (New York, 1929), p. 66.

were shrewd buyers, had more money to spend than their stay-at-home sisters, and greater need to spend it. Thus, the economic power of this group meant that working women increasingly became the standard-setters for other women in dress. Whether or not they bought a particular design in their lunch-hour shopping expeditions to the downtown stores could make or break a manufacturer, or a retailer.

Contemporaries were well aware that the entrance of women into the business world in large numbers was producing a radical change in clothing. For example, a home economics teacher wrote in 1926 that

> With the entrance of women into the business world the demand came for comfortable dress which did not hamper the wearer in any way, and would hold its own no matter in what situation its owner found herself. It must have lasting qualities as well, for the business woman, like the business man, must not be bothered with constant repairs. It must be easy to put on. The designers set to work and the one-piece slip on gown was the result.[4]

All of which is true enough, and, indeed, the importance of the timesaving factor cannot be overemphasized. But the need for a change in clothing derived from more than the simple fact that now many women were working for a living and before they had not been.

Edward Sapir characterized woman as traditionally understood as "the one who pleases by being what she is and looking as she does rather than by doing what she does." As the "kept partner in marriage," she used fashion to emphasize perpetually her desirability. She was a status symbol, an "expensive luxury."[5] Veblen's analysis of fashion, from which

Sapir took off, applied very specifically to the Gibson girl.

According to Veblen, the importance of clothing is that one's expenditures on dress are always out where they can be plainly seen. Fashion is thus a popular and universal outlet for conspicuous display, especially since failure to come up to expected standards in this area can be mortifying. Thus, too, clothing's commercial value is largely determined by its fashionableness rather than by its utility. It is fashionable clothing that communicates to the onlooker what the wearer wants known about himself, that he is wealthy, nonproductive and leisured. For women especially, clothing demonstrates that the wearer does not and need not work and, indeed, cannot because of the impracticality of her attire, such as long hair, large hats, high-heeled shoes, elaborate skirts and draperies, corsets and so on. For Veblen then, the Gibson girl's femininity was bound up in her inability to do anything useful, symbolized and reinforced by her dress.

The Gibson girl was the manikin for the fashionable clothing which testified to her husband's ability to free her from work and on whom he hung the symbols of his prosperity. She was in this sense responsible for the "good name" of her household, living testimony to its economic as well as its moral respectability; this was her job. For the Gibson girl her grooming itself was her profession; to be her husband's "prized possession" was her career.

But in the postwar years many women were no longer content with this role of expensive chattel nor with the physical, economic, social and sexual limitations which it imposed on their lives. Many women could no longer "be satisfied with their [husbands'] esteem and with such agreeable objects as homes, gardens, and

---

[4] Sage, p. 215.
[5] Edward Sapir, "Fashion," in *Encyclopedia of the Social Sciences* (New York, 1931), VI, 142.

pretty clothes."[6] For one thing, the work environment itself induced many women to shift their emphasis toward practicality in dress. Energy was channeled into social modes of behavior. A premium was put on correct behavior and attire for the social situation, while less value was placed on attractiveness alone.

Thus it was possible to write in 1930 that "There seems to be . . . no essential factor in the nature, habits, or functions of the two sexes that would necessitate a striking difference of costume—other than the desire to accentuate sex differences themselves. . . ."[7] The tendency in the 1920s was toward the blurring of many such differences in dress. This drive toward greater simplicity and practicability in dress gained impetus from the change in life style that many women underwent. The advances and demands of technology enabled women to get the kind of clothing they needed. The growth of the sporting life had a similar effect. Tennis could not be played in croquet costume, any more than business could be conducted effectively in parlor dress. For women, athletics, like business, was no longer quite the frivolous matter it had been, and women brought a new seriousness to dress.

The economic independence that came with jobs meant that there were fewer "dependent women," either daughters or wives. The sacred institutions of the home and the family were being eroded: "For city dwellers the home was steadily becoming less of a shrine, more of a dormitory."[8] Women now dressed, not for doting fathers or loving husbands, but for the competitive arena and a social situation. While for the housewife such situations may be more or less infrequent, the career woman is exposed to them daily; she is continually surrounded and observed by her male and female peers and superiors.

The new office situation made constant demands on women and necessitated a dress and grooming appropriate for it. Perfumes as well as natural body odors, for example, had to be minimal in "the enforced intimacy of heterosexual office work," so that the "physical being" may be de-emphasized and "the social role and the office" stressed. Sexuality had to be understated in order for the work of the office to continue smoothly. The career woman had to "conceal and control" her femininity, to "reduce herself to an *office*" by minimizing her "natural shape, smell, color, texture, and movement and to replace these by impersonal, neutral surfaces."[9] Hence, for example, the popularity of the colors black and beige in the 1920s.

While sexuality never disappears in the office situation it is usually muted and controlled, turned "from a raw physical relationship to a civilized game."[10] The exposure of some parts of the body does not contradict this principle. The parts exposed were those most remote from the explicitly sexual areas, while the waist was lowered and the breast bound to make their existence and exact location matters of some guesswork. The lowering of the forehead, shaping of eyebrows and emphasis on make-up tended, among other things, to make the eyes appear larger, more "battable," stressing the seductive, coquettish aspects of sexuality. Finally, it

---

[6] Winifred Raushenbush, "The Idiot God Fashion," in *Woman's Coming of Age*, eds. Samuel D. Schmalhausen and V. F. Calverton (New York, 1931), p. 442.

[7] Flügel, p. 201.

[8] Frederick Lewis Allen, *Only Yesterday* (New York, 1964), p. 81.

---

[9] Murray Wax, "Themes in Cosmetics and Grooming" in Roach and Eicher, p. 39.

[10] Ibid, pp. 42–45.

has been argued that exposure removes the aura of mystery which clothing lends to the female body, thereby making it possible for both sexes to concentrate on business, sexual curiosity and urge to display satisfied.

The office became a kind of hunting ground in which males were captured and tamed in their native habitat. But it was more important that a proper uniform for the office as social situation be devised. Clothes are a kind of communication, establishing a relationship between wearer and observer before a word has been exchanged. They evoke, if properly used, a predictable set of responses concerning identity, values, moods and attitudes. The importance of dress to the hurried world of business thus becomes clear: it can be a useful shortcut to acquiring information about others and telling them about oneself. One knows whom he is dealing with even in the most fleeting contact, what the hierarchies are and the status of persons on a day-to-day basis. Clothes, as a social uniform, identify the players and the name of the game as well.

The working woman, married or not, had a big economic edge over the non-working woman, which she could use in sexual competition as well, aided by her greater proximity to men, her presence in the male arena. This put a great deal of pressure on women who did not have jobs to seek them. Moreover, there were often family economic needs compelling them to do so. Most growing families could use more money, and parents are able to spend less and less money on themselves as their children grow older, until the children become self-supporting. The long-term trend has been for families to have fewer children and for women to have them earlier in life so as to be able to return to work at the time of the family's greatest economic need.

Most observers in the 1920s remarked that the housewife herself seemed to be emerging toward emancipation. Smaller, centrally heated houses were easier to clean, and many other families lived in apartments. Canned and frozen foods began to dominate the American diet, along with store-brought baked goods. Out-of-home housekeeping services and the availability of inexpensive mechanical and electrical devices in the home also tended to ease the housewife's burden. But the liberation of the housewife had just begun in the 1920s, hardly approaching the proportions it would later assume.

Nevertheless, the housewife's emancipation had gone sufficiently far to cause some concern in Middletown for the diffusion of activities once centered about the home. Technological advances were accepted, but always with a proviso: "fresh encroachments tend to be met by a reassertion of the traditional *noli tangere* attitude toward the 'sacred institution' of the home." At Middletown's Chautauqua, a speaker observed:

We seem to be drifting away from the fundamentals in our home life. The home was once a sacred institution where the family spent most of its time. Now it is a physical service station except for the old and the infirm.[11]

If many people were wary and worried about where it would all end, women, by and large, seemed pleased that the boundaries of their universe now extended past the front gate.

Clothes were not only the symbol of this partial emancipation, but one of the tools which made it possible as well. As one woman wrote to *The Literary Digest:*

Think of the ease of laundering the simple modern clothes, and of the time saved in fitting. Manufacturers turn out gowns in

---

[11] Robert S. and Helen M. Lynd, *Middletown* (New York, 1929), pp. 177–78.

sizes by the gross, and almost any figure can wear them with little or no alteration.[12]

The impact of ready-made clothing on Middletown's home life was a reflection of the growth of the ready-to-wear clothing industry in America. The uneven movement of this sector of the economy toward rationalization pointed to a time not too far off when all Americans could be well- and fashionably-dressed within weeks of the debut of styles in Paris or New York. One expert remarked that the consumer no longer needed to be concerned overmuch with utility, durability or colorfastness when purchasing clothing; mass production, he argued rather sanguinely, enabled manufacturers to ensure the quality of their products.

The combined effects of rationalization and prosperity had facilitated the diffusion of fashions and increased the market for them. Moreover, the high initial profits accruing from the introduction of a successful design put a premium on rapid and thorough distribution, quick turnover and the marketing of new styles as soon as they were born. Had it not been for large inventories, this process might have been even more rapid than it was.

Clothes-making, once a function of the home and the job of the homemaker, had now become clothes-buying, dependent on the family's or individual's earning power. The Lynds reported that as late as 1910, newspaper advertisements for yard goods had been numerous in Middletown, while there had been almost none for ready-made dresses. By the 1920s the position was reversed.

The rise of the jobbing system, lending some rationality to the industry, was not favorable to the formerly common individualism and creativity. But it seemed perfectly well suited to the new, simpler

styles. So, too, did mechanization. If the emphasis on cost-cutting reduced opportunities for individual workmanship, the popular modes left little room for such virtuosity in any case. Both the industry and the market moved toward simple, stylish, ready-made garments made quickly and distributed rapidly. The Sears, Roebuck catalogue for the fall-winter, 1929–30, featured a dress described in these terms:

Paris Sends You This Dress In the Smartest French Manner. . . .

From Paris to you . . . speeded across the ocean . . . rushed to our style studios in the heart of New York . . . Reproduced with deft rapidity . . . Adapted with exquisite skill to the needs and tastes of American women . . . *Parisian Style!!*

Mass production was manufacturing luxury for all: Paris originals, in two colors, available to all of the tens of thousands of women who wanted them, for only $10.95, postpaid.

Perhaps the greatest single fact that had made all of this possible was the implementation of the idea that women came in sizes, seven of which would fit half the women in the country. A bell-shaped distribution about two of the sizes was manufactured and bought by the department stores, a very efficient and profitable way of dressing the women of America.

The sizes developed were especially good for young figures, which is perhaps further explanation of the emphasis in this period on youthful styles: "It is estimated that approximately 90% of the young people between the ages of fifteen to nineteen may be fitted by the standard sizes for these ages, that about half the adults from 20 to 44 may be cared for with standard sizes, but that only a third of the population from the age of 45 up may be properly fitted with such standard

[12] "Today's Morals and Manners—The Side of 'The Girls'," *The Literary Digest,* LXX, 36.

sizes."[13] It seemed that technology was peculiarly suited to the needs of the young woman.

Although mass production in the apparel industry in the 1920s gave impetus to the drive toward simplicity and uniformity, it also worked in the direction of variety and multiplicity. It now became possible to offer consumers at reasonable prices a wide range of fabrics, textures, colors and styles, and also a greater number of types of garments, that is, clothing suited for specific occasions and needs, such as formal evening wear, town and afternoon dresses and suits, business wear, sports outfits, work clothing and many others. This diversification, and the diffusion of fashionable clothing, too, had the effect of breaking down the patent outward manifestations of class: "Only a connoisseur can distinguish Miss Astorbilt on Fifth Avenue from her father's stenographer or secretary.[14]

But the industry which had worked such a miracle on the face of America seemed utterly vulnerable to something called fashion, over which it had little control. Carried far forward and, alternately, overwhelmed by its uncharted ebbs and flows, the ready-to-wear industry was more victim than giant. It seemed unwilling to adapt for its own needs the marketing techniques (notably market research) which had gone so far toward regularizing the automobile industry, among others, in the 1920s. If fashion could be controlled, American manufacturers were not the manipulators. The obvious place to look for the men pulling the threads is Paris.

The French clothing industry held roughly the same position in the French economy that the automobile industry now occupies in the United States. The establishments ranged from highly individualistic and creative to a very few mass production operations on the American model. Each of the 25 largest houses alone accounted for from 500 to 1000 new designs annually.

But the size of the industry did not disguise its lack of modernity. It relied almost entirely on accumulated prestige, the originality of its designers and the manual proficiency of the French seamstress. France was ill-equipped to compete with American mechanization in the large-volume production of simple styles; it hoped and agitated for the return of the more detailed, elaborate styles which would bestow the advantage once more to its skilled workers. The flapper, American in origin, was a bitter pill for the Parisian couturiers to swallow. Though partly sold to the world by Paris' prestige, this same prestige was put behind annual efforts to dethrone the flapper, efforts which did not succeed until 1930.

After World War I, Paris was faced with an unprecedented demand from a new clientele more interested in the correctness than the uniqueness of its dress. This, and the tubular silhouette, forced Paris to give up its emphasis on exclusiveness. Much of this financial pressure came from America and the incentive to sell to American manufacturers for duplication here was very great; the old fears of style piracy were overcome. Paris found itself reproducing its own models for sale to manufacturers all over the world. Several of the most successful Parisian houses got that way precisely because of their ability to sell in the American market. This was true of Lelong, Chanel, Premet and Patou, whose adoption of American modes and sales techniques led them to dominance of the French domestic and export markets.

In fact, Paris' more dismal moments

---

[13] Paul H. Nystrom, *Economics of Fashion* (New York, 1928), p. 463.
[14] Chase, p. 65.

came at precisely those times when it tried to buck American trends. The most notorious example was Paris' reaction to the short skirt, which it detested. During the depression of 1921–22, Paris predicted unequivocally that the short skirt was on its way out and that the straight silhouette would be altered as well. The reaction of the American industry to these pronouncements was characteristically sheeplike. Textile mills rejoiced at the anticipated use of greater yardage, while apparel manufacturers distributed garments with longer skirts to their customers, the wholesalers and retailers who, in turn, tried to pass them off on the consumer.

But American women weren't having any. Sales of garments with longer skirts slowed drastically while women hunted for the shorter ones. If they did buy the longer-skirted dresses they wore them once and then had them altered more to their liking at the retailers' expense. Throughout the fall of 1923 and the spring of 1924 the complaints of retailers whose alteration expenses were skyrocketing could be heard all the way to Paris. Thereafter, skirts continued their uninterrupted rise until they reached the top of the knee in 1927.

This debacle had several less disastrous but equally intriguing counterparts. Throughout the 1920s, Paris predicted year in and year out that wider hats would be in, but they were always out. Every year between 1921 and 1928 the return of the tailored suit was heralded, but it never caught on. One observer commented with marked understatement that prewar claims to "fashion dictatorship" by several Parisian couturiers had been moderated by postwar developments.

But if Paris was no dictator, the relative success of the great skirt counter-revolution of 1929–30 becomes an intriguing problem. The chronology is straightforward enough. In 1928, Paris started a series of inroads on the dominant styles: an occasional head replaced the cloche with a turban or a wider brim; the austere tubular chemise dress had been embellished with bows and panels, *godets* and shirring; the straight high hem was superseded by an uneven one of "dripping, flaring panels or slithering trains of ribbon width dangling below." During the summer of 1929 in the showings of fall fashions by the Paris houses skirts plummeted toward the floor. One observer at Patou's first show that season reported that "All the women are squirming about in their chairs, tugging at their skirts. Already they feel *démodée*."[15]

It was not that easy to make American women at home feel uncomfortable with what they were wearing. The gradual incursions on the flapper mode had met with signs of awakening resistance. *The New York Times,* for example, noted "the general disinclination to follow the dictum of Paris that shirts be longer" among the marchers in the 1929 Easter parade.

The evidence for considering 1929 as a kind of transitional year in the dominant female aesthetic is suggestive rather than strong, but is worth noting. Apparently women were willing to modify the prevailing mode but manufacturers, burnt several times before, were unsure of their ability to predict the relative acceptability of a change and tried to follow events.

The industry was warned that it would not prove easy to sell garments in the new style. The Merchandise and Research Bureau predicted resistance to the longer skirt and the new waistline and urged the trade to put special emphasis on the changes to make them more palatable. A merchandiser advised putting stress

---

[15] Edna Woolman Chase and Ilka Chase, *Always in Vogue* (New York, 1954), pp. 213 ff.

on the trend "toward a more formal way of living" and the desire to have clothes with "more of a made to order look." Such talk, however, apparently did little to instill confidence among the retailers of the salability of the new styles: "Retailers as yet are on the fence waiting for the consumer response to indicate their buying policies."[16]

It was not long before resistance materialized. Revealed in the columns of *The New York Times* in letters to the editor, news stories and editorials, this resistance showed high sophistication, that is, an awareness of what clothing — especially the modes of the 1920s — represented to the wearer. Lucie R. Saylor's letter, which drew much support, merits lengthy citation:

It has taken many centuries of hard, slow struggle to attain the present degree of freedom from cumbersome feminine clothes. If we women are willing to give up that freedom and the moral victory it represents just because Parisian modistes issue arbitrary decrees and manufacturers want to sell more materials, we are scarcely worthy to have the vote and other hard-won modern liberties. Ankle-length skirts and confining waists — and the minds of those willing to wear them — belong to the Middle Ages or to the harem.

Several other female *Times* readers agreed. E. B. C. added that while the "society woman" or "grande dame" of whom little movement was required might be able to wear "Long, trailing gowns of fragile silks and velvets, trimmed with real lace . . . what about the hordes of women and girls who travel in the subways and work in offices?"[17]

The revolt was sufficiently serious to warrant a *New York Times Magazine*

article on it. Noting that Paris had chosen "femininity" at the expense of "comfort or bank accounts" the author went on to say that feminine was meant "in its narrowest and most thoroughly traditional sense," a sense irrelevant to American women in 1929 but keyed to an idealization of French women before the fall, *i.e.,* their contamination by modern ideas. The French couturiers had indulged in "an orgy of nostalgia." But this same article struck an ambivalent note: "It would look as though women were persuaded that they were tired of simplicity and bored with freedom" and ready to accept a greater formality in some aspects or types of dress, especially evening wear. This hint of indecisiveness as to which role she wanted to play or perhaps her desire to play both if possible may be a vital clue toward an understanding of the American woman's ultimate acceptance of a more "feminine" costume.

The uncertainty continued over the winter. The *Times* observed that while the new modes were bought they were not worn except for formal evening wear. The Women's Federation sponsored a debate on the subject of skirt lengths whose outcome was predictably inconclusive. Manufacturers were likewise insecure. J. J. Goldman, founder of Associated Dress Industries, reported that the long skirt was curtailing sales, but predicted that it would be accepted by spring. A showing of New York designs for the spring, held more than a month before the Paris exhibitions to demonstrate independence, was conciliatory in intent, setting the length at six inches below the knee and moderating other extreme measures taken in the fall. A partial retreat was in evidence as well in the spring-summer shows in Paris, but this was evidently not rapid enough to please American manufacturers and merchandisers who by now had become angry with Paris' inability or un-

[16] New York *Times,* Aug. 4, 1929, II, p. 8; Aug. 6, 1929, p. 42; Sept. 1, 1929, II, p. 14.

[17] New York *Times,* Sept. 7, 1929, p. 16; Sept. 9, 1929, p. 24; Sept. 30, 1929, p. 30.

willingness to develop clothes salable on the American market. The most recent experience in bucking consumer tastes at Paris' behest was too much: "Our endorsement of the very long skirt and the bizarre details last Fall," said Henry H. Finder, former President of the Industrial Council of Cloak, Suit and Skirt Manfacturers, Inc., "was a serious and costly mistake and we shall not permit it to occur again."

Nevertheless, it was obvious that Paris had finally succeeded in doing what it had wanted to do all along: it had finally made the longer skirt stick. The Sears catalogues, starting with spring-summer 1930, reflected the winter compromises and were dominated by the new styles, with longer and fuller skirts, re-emphasized bust, waist and hips, tailored suits, prints and patterns, and larger hats. But the change had occurred *in* the American market. Some hypotheses on the nature of fashion may help illuminate these changes.

Although the machine threatened to obliterate class distinctions in dress, in a way it also helped to maintain them. The fact that of two identical garments one was mass-produced while the other was an "original" made by hand continued to give great prestige to the owner of the latter article: "The aesthetic value of a detected counterfeit in dress declines somewhat in the same proportion as the counterfeit is cheaper than its original."[18] The spread of fashion through a community is a function of the size of the middle class, which feels urgently the need to distinguish itself from the rest of the population. Thus the fashion cycle gains impetus from the drive of members of key affluent groups to emulate their superiors and dissociate themselves from their inferiors; the larger the middle class, the more rapid the turnover of modes.

Talking about groups makes it easy to forget that a large number of individual decisions are involved which are made on the basis of personal circumstances, relationships and needs. Fashion is a way of enabling individuals to belong where they want to belong, and to cut themselves off from undesired associations. It is an instrument of social mobility. Moreover, it is a legitimized outlet for personal self-expression, particularly valuable for persons who feel they live in a society in which the individual is devalued. Fashion is a kind of safety valve for aberrant individual or group tendencies, such as, in the 1920s, class consciousness in a democratic society, sexual curiosity in a puritanical one or individuality in a mass culture.

New fashions, of course, do not always find favor with the fashion following; certain conditions have to be met by the style itself and by the persons proposing it. A style which is too far out of the mainstream of public values, which satisfies neither articulated nor inarticulate needs, is liable to be abandoned quickly or not taken up at all. This happened to the harem skirt, proposed in the 1910s, which apparently failed to pick up support because it symbolized an extreme form of the subjugation women were trying to escape. The farther out a style is, moreover, the greater the prestige needed by the initiator to make it catch on, but even the most modest innovation needs someone of stature behind it. What form of prestige is necessary varies according to social circumstances. By the 1920s the days of royal fashion plates were over and movie stars seemed to have replaced them as the great influences on American women.

This is no frivolous matter. The deci-

---

[18] Thorstein Veblen, *The Theory of the Leisure Class* (New York, 1934), p. 169.

sion that a woman makes to follow one fashion leader and not another means that one has spoken to some important need and the other has not. When this process is repeated several million times, *i.e.*, sufficiently often to become a fashion trend, then we are dealing not with individual variations and impulses but with what amounts to a major social movement in which aesthetic and moral values are undergoing drastic and rapid change. On the surface this process seems to go on effortlessly. But previous to the change many women had to be groping about, feeling dissatisfied (perhaps unconsciously) with what they were wearing, wishing for some style of clothing that expressed *them* better, their needs and their aspirations. Having undergone what amounts to a change in identity by the 1920s many women needed a change of costume in order better to communicate what they thought about themselves and wanted thought about them, who they were.

CHARLOTTE PERKINS GILMAN (1860–1935) was among the foremost intellectuals in the woman movement. Her best known work, *Women And Economics* (1898), is still a telling analysis of the problem. Here, in one of her last published writings, she raised questions about the effects of sexual freedom which remain unanswered even though the revolution has gone far beyond what anyone then imagined.*

Charlotte Perkins Gilman

A Dissent

There is no more basic essential to social advance than the economic processes of production and distribution. Progressing normally this should mean the widest development of talent and skill, and the widest distribution of product among the people. This natural social progress has been always interfered with by the persistence of a grossly disproportionate individualism, and that individualism has been maintained, at great disadvantage to society, by our excessive and misplaced sex development.

The woman service which was of such advantage to the early male soon grew into slave service, a status which has dominated the economic field throughout all history, and the influence of which, with its associated emotions, still prejudices the popular mind against work. It is true that possession of the dependent woman has acted as a spur to man's energies, but his effort was to secure for her, as well as for himself and children, as much as he could get.

Instead of a normal social distribution which would ensure to all the nourishment essential to full production, we have had a world of struggling men trying to get away from one another the products of their industry, a world of destructive competition. It is no wonder that with socialist and communist theories there is associated in the popular mind

* Excerpted from Charlotte Perkins Gilman, article originally entitled "Sex and Race Progress," in V. F. Calverton and S. D. Schmalhausen, *Sex in Civilization* (New York: Macaulay, 1929), pp. 118–123. Reprinted by permission of Mrs. Katherine Stetson Chamberlin and the Arthur and Elizabeth Schlesinger Library on the History of Women in America.

49

the fear of sex promiscuity. Seeing women as possessions, and assuming common ownership of all property, it is natural, for minds accustomed to believe and not to think, to entertain this confused idea.

As a matter of fact promiscuity, such as was found in declining Rome, for instance, is no mark of communism, but of sex decay. Perhaps no better proof of our misuse of function can be shown than in this very tendency toward promiscuity which has accompanied the advance of civilization and contributed to its repeated ruin.

As an animal species we are monogamous, like many others. But natural distinctions are not immovable, and under pressure of circumstances we have become in some races polygamous, in a few instances polyandrous, and in certain stages of culture, promiscuous. At present there seems to be quite a general reversion toward promiscuity, accompanied with a new theory of the essential need of sex indulgence at all costs.

If this is to produce better members of society, or conduce to social progress, it is justified, but as far as the promiscuity goes it uses the most careful measures to avoid producing anything; and in the matter of social progress we have yet to see if these sex enthusiasts are therefore stronger, wiser, more skillful in human activities.

If the relation which makes sex indulgence either openly purchasable, or at best, requires ability to secure *support* for a family, puts a heavy emphasis on the predatory instincts of men, and often flatly controverts their social instincts, what is the effect on women, in relation to race progress?

The mother instinct, socialized, is clearly seen at work in the peace, industry, order and wealth of ant and bee. The mother instinct, personalized, is a limitless devotion to one's own family. Women, having been debarred from socialization in its wide legitimate processes of production and distribution, and their activities confined to intimate personal service, have found a meager outlet in what they call "society"—(a sort of children's party) and in the well-meant but illegitimate processes of "charity."

In genuine advance they have had small part, with occasional exceptions in favored periods and places, until the present time. Now they are emerging from their previous restrictions and engaging more and more freely in the genuine social processes of specialized activity.

But so far this enlargement is seen as "self-expression," and neither as members of society nor as a sex is there any general recognition of power to promote the progress of the race. That power is so preeminently theirs that we may hope for a marked acceleration in improvement when it is realized.

The influence of sex on race progress, to promote which is its original purpose, has a range and depth of action never yet utilized in humanity. Because of our artificially extended and enforced individualism we are slow to admit the application of this immense power to determined improvement.

Each woman, engrossed in her own children, feels some responsibility for their inherited physique and character, and a little more for their "bringing up." But the women of a country do not yet face their responsibility for the children of that country and their right rearing.

Among our many popular misconceptions as to the nature of sex is one amusing contradiction. We are willing to trace sex-distinction through physical and psychic attributes, and out into such superficial distinctions as those of dress and occupation; with men we have unquestioningly attributed all their superior achievements to their sex.

Yet when an improved system of education, a more beneficial service through government, or increased public care of children, is shown as an extension of social motherhood, a sex function, we stoutly deny it. Motherhood we admit as a not too-necessary consequence of mating, but it is the mating itself most men mean when they talk of sex. It is not surprising, in a masculine culture, that this should be so; with the male the process culminates in that preliminary. With the female it goes on through increasingly elaborate functions.

There is an amusing absurdity in this exaltation of the match that lights the fire, while minimizing the cookstove and the dinner. These big books and little books, these lectures and classes, this endless discussion of sex which palls upon the ear to-day, is almost wholly confined to the brief preliminary, the primitive initial step, of this tremendous process.

But while natural for the male to overestimate the importance of his small share in a great undertaking, it is ridiculous for the female. When she says "sex" it should mean to her the whole of her great power. This is something far beyond that boasted "sex-appeal." To appeal, to attract, to secure a mate, to consummate that attraction, this, all told, is the merest beginning. If the love that lasts through life goes with it, there is the highest personal happiness we know. If children follow, well-loved and well reared, there is more personal happiness and personal duty.

But human beings are more than persons, they are members of society. If men, for self-indulgence, maintain what has

been called a "necessary institution," prostitution, they injure society. The large number of women so misused are deprived of home and family, denied motherhood, and also kept out of social productivity, a dead loss. Here is the sex with the larger share in a great function balked of its real use and made to contribute to the temporary enjoyment of the lesser actor in the process, while even his contribution is totally useless.

It needs no Puritan or moralist of any sort to criticize this absurd relationship. It was just as absurd when considered a virtue as when considered a sin, when considered a necessity as when seen to be a gross injury to society as well as the participants. If we are ever to appreciate sex at its true value it will be only by recognizing the whole of it, and not by overestimating a part of it.

As our history stands, we can see clearly enough how much this vital impulse has contributed to race progress, in so far as it improved the stock, or increased the value of individuals. We can see its lovely heights in types of undying love, in instances of parental devotion. No matter how wrongly we may conceive it, a natural force cannot be utterly thwarted even by our mistakes.

That we are still here, and on the whole advancing, shows that those mistakes have not been fatal. But when we look at our best progress, in the most advanced races, when we see the kind of people we produce and their manifold sufferings, it does seem as if we might do better in the way of progress.

While freely admitting the power and value of sex when naturally used, with the higher and subtler development of this function in our species, and even some advantages pursuant upon our misuse of it, the record of race progress clearly shows how our upward movement has been checked, perverted, often brought to an end, by that misuse.

To it is traceable the mischievous persistence of an exaggerated individualism in our economics, an individualism whose more than natural greed is stimulated by the limitless demands of the dependent women, married or hired. With a normal sex life, with women functioning socially as well as sexually, we should be able to recognize the immense advantages of orderly cooperation in production and distribution, the disadvantages of fierce competition, the worst effect of which is war.

That ultra-masculine competition, so useful in its original form when it meant the triumph of the personally superior, is anything but an advantage when it means only the triumph of the richer, and when the riches are acquired by faculties not socially advantageous. Race progress requires the appearance of highly specialized talents in arts and sciences, and highly developed cooperation in industry and business, and those most gifted in such lines are by no means always most gifted in sex.

The weak point in our present tendency to deify sex as the source of all our superiorities is that no evidence is produced to show that those most advanced in socially serviceable qualities are also most strongly sexed. The difference in degree of development in sex is perforce admitted, with a frank admiration of those showing most of it; we are further told of this or that eminent man who was or is highly sexed, with no mention of those lacking, but it cannot be shown that the world's greatest servants are also greatest sexually.

On the other hand there are plenty of cases of highly sexed persons who are not high in anything else, and many more where the excess in this power is accompanied by distinctly detrimental qualities. We need evidence, accurately observed and carefully recorded, showing the relation of large development in this power with commensurate development in those human distinctions which conduce to social progress. Such evidence would not involve the *rationalized* hypothesis that our most unsexual activities are but the product of *sublimated* sex.

The basic use of sex in human advance should be in the conscious improvement of the species. We need it. Women, whose share in this work is so far the greatest, should face it as their main responsibility. The elimination of the unfit is a necessary part of that responsibility; already approached in some places by enforced sterilization of grossly injurious types. The development of the fit requires a far more intelligent selection than an admiration for sex-appeal.

However much the male may be preoccupied with his contribution, the female should feel her tremendous power for lifting the quality of the human race, and use it. It would take but a few generations to outgrow our present morbid development, especially when false and artificial opinions are changed.

There would remain to us the natural use and enjoyment of this function, now so often unattainable; and the equally natural but far higher development of mutual love in a race normally monogamous, and having an ever increasing area of attachment. A human creature has more to love in his mate, or hers, than the most devoted pair of swans.

There is no more necessary step to preserve and promote race progress than the recognition of the right purpose and power of sex and its full use.

It is admittedly difficult to measure human happiness, but if we may judge at all by the faces of the old, those who have enjoyed a lifelong companionship with one genuine love, show marks of contentment not found in those who have had the widest range in sex contacts. Nor does that happiness seem relative to intensity or frequency in indulgence, but rather to perfect accord.

Our condition is too feverish, our relations too artificial and hitherto too unjust, for happiness in marriage to be frequent. But when it is found, it is difficult to parallel by happiness in "free union," however often repeated.

In a relation so preeminently individual, personal happiness is a main requirement. In a sex-ridden world, with a dominant male, it has not been generally secured. The various laws and customs with which he has tried to govern this relation have not made him contented with it, to say nothing of her. Early chapters in the misuse of women were so detrimental to the stock as to extinguish some races and keep others at the lowest level, bare reproduction with no progress.

The thin stream of continuity might have been thus expressed by that misused primitive female:

> I lived and bore
> And, though I died,
> So that I lived to bear,
> My daughter lived and bore.

All this cruelty we have outgrown. The more recent disadvantages of matrimony are being rectified rapidly. Knowledge of sex is replacing the unhealthy ignorance once thought necessary. The freedom of women, with their swift growth in human qualities, allows of a larger appreciation of their power than is as yet shown.

That they have become over-sexed, even more than men, was inevitable in their previous condition. However self-indulgent were men, they had also the whole range of human activities wherein to function; while women had no avenue of expression, aside from the arrested domestic labors and the most limited maternal ones, save this main field of the eternal feminine.

Since every condition of their lives developed sex, and yet, with admirable logic and justice, they were forbidden the expression allowed to men, it is no wonder that in their sudden freedom they astonish many by their excesses. It is not possible that a morbid condition, developed through ages of misuse, should revert to a natural one in a generation.

Our disproportionate urge of sex is to be treated with understanding and patience, not with condemnation. It is a pity that an abnormal state should be reinforced by an abnormal philosophy, but that too will be outgrown. Most needed is an understanding by women of the overwhelming importance of their own sex, in its wide and prolonged activities, in its indispensable value to race progress; in place of our ridiculous preoccupation with sex from the male point of view, where all attention is concentrated on the power and pleasure of sex union.

All that power and pleasure will remain to us, all the limitless exaltation of mutual love; but when normal relations are established we shall have also peace and health for the individual, and the sure foundation for a swifter and smoother social advance than the world has ever seen.

DOROTHY D. BROMLEY and FLORENCE H. BRITTEN were journalists at the time they investigated the sexual standards of college students. Although social scientists were beginning to apply more rigorous standards in this area, this amateur study was intelligently and sensitively done. Are the sex lives of college students today much different from what they were in the 1930s? Allowing for different tastes in clothes, social functions, and the like, is it possible to measure the one period against the other? How does one separate the outward appearances from the inner substance of the college culture?*

Dorothy D. Bromley and Florence H. Britten

The Sex Lives of College Students

Clear-minded young people are mystified by the prudishness lingering about sex. They look at pictures of women's bathing-suits in the 90's and try to understand the motives for such "quaint" costumes. Taking for granted the freedom of sun suits and shorts for both sexes, they wonder at the persistent tendency to consider the human body nasty. They cannot understand why New York City customs officials should have held up within the last decade, photographs of Michelangelo's frescoes on the ceiling of the Sistine Chapel in the Vatican, labeling them "obscene photo books."

When the young people examine their elders' social behavior, they discover very poor performance in comparison with prudish pretension. They scarcely need to read vital statistics to learn that one marriage in every six or seven ends in the divorce courts. The effects of broken homes among their playmates has taught the younger generation, while still in the nursery, something of the breakdown of family life.

The Problem of Prolonged Celibacy

Another paradox of the prevailing sex mores moves the younger generation to impatience. In recent years the American standard of living has risen

* From pp. 7–21 in *Youth and Sex* by Dorothy Dunbar Bromley and Florence Haxton Britten. Copyright 1938 by Harper & Row, Publishers, Inc. Reprinted by permission of Harper & Row, Publishers, Inc. Most footnotes omitted.

so sharply as to make a young man increasingly hesitant to ask a girl to share the penury of his first years out of college. An even more difficult situation is the tendency of our society to demand more and more years in school of those who want to get ahead. Graduate training was formerly limited to the learned professions of law and medicine and to the non-evangelical clergy. Today, for anyone above the rank of unskilled laborer, lack of a college degree is an embarrassment, and two to four years of graduate work beckon the ambitious into schools of engineering, business management, and other specialized lines.

While the country has doubled its population since 1890, the number of college and graduate students has multiplied 12 times. Today one per cent of the country's entire population are college students. These figures reflect not only the rising standard of living, but they mean also that all the thousands of college men who fall in love must be torn between the ambition to fit themselves for their life work and their desire to marry.

Some people take an especial delight in anything unnatural and forced, such as fish and game out of season. Veblen long ago discussed this tendency in his law of conspicuous waste. Civilization seems to take a similar perverse pleasure in forcing human beings into difficult and unnatural situations. Our boys and girls normally attain puberty between the ages of twelve and sixteen. It is increasingly difficult for them to marry before they are twenty-two to twenty-six. During the years that the mating urge is strongest young people find ever additional obstacles blocking their way. Our mores make no concession by offering them legitimate means of sex expression. One student phrased the situation

with forceful resentment. "Why," he asked, "does the older generation create a society which makes normal gratification very difficult and then criticize us for acting normally?" Another scornfully referred to the established code of the older generation as "their silly moralistic conventions which are truly immoral in so far as their attitude toward our youthful passions is concerned."

Traditional morality has presupposed that the rigors of celibacy will present no grave problem to young men and women until a mystical moment, sanctified by social usage, releases them into an unbounded license. It is not surprising that the more adventuresome young people, unhappily impaled on the horns of a biological dilemma, are frankly experimenting and working out their own trial-and-error solutions. Noting their elders' inconsistencies, thoughtful young men and women are carried by the swift current of a college life far ahead into a field of alert and detached skepticism. It is this skepticism which marks an important distinction between the jazz-mad 20's and the willful but soberer 30's.

Changing Sex Mores

Young people impatient of old traditions may find encouragement in the fact that their elders have for some time been quietly involved in a revision of their own sex mores. After all, the wayward schoolgirl of Judge Lindsey's *Revolt of Modern Youth* is today a woman of thirty. The report of the Committee on Recent Social Trends included an interesting study by Dr. Hornell Hart of changing moral codes as indicated by the popular attitude toward extramarital sex relations. It undertook to measure the actual change registered since the turn of the century by those sensitive thermometers, the popular-fiction magazines and the movies. Statistical analysis of plots of all stories appearing in a large group of popular magazines showed that in the period of 1900–05 only 3 per cent of the plots condoned the hero's or heroine's extramarital sex relations. By contrast, the movie and magazine plots of 1932 condoned such relations in 45 percent of the cases. The study concluded that popular tolerance of extramarital sex relations is several times as great as it was in 1900.

A recent popular survey also evidenced widespread reaction from the stern morality of yesterday. *Fortune's* Quarterly Survey in 1937 sent out investigators to ring doorbells and ask questions on sex standards. One question was, "Do you think it all right for either or both parties to a marriage to have had previous sexual experience?"

It indicates a change of temper that the average citizen should be willing to come to his front door and frankly discuss such intimate questions with strange canvassers. Summarizing the answers received, *Fortune* said, "The first observation that springs to eye is the weakness of the approval for the double standard. Old or young, three out of every four non-believers in strict premarital purity believe that women are entitled equally with men to sexual experience." Nearly one-quarter (22.3 per cent) of all those questioned approved of pre-marital sexual experience for both men and women.

Paradoxically, more than half of the people questioned were opposed to easy divorce laws. There was a widespread desire to protect the institution of marriage; yet a not inconsiderable minority felt that the old-fashioned demand for pre-marital continence is impractical and cannot be enforced, even among women.

A Factory Frankenstein

Various long-range social changes have contributed to the sabotage of established sex mores. The basic material event in this process has been the invention of machines and the spread of the factory system. Factories with their insatiable demand for cheap labor near at hand have crowded the population into urban centers. The sophisticated and the vicious influences of city life have alike been antagonistic to the old conventional codes of sex mores.

The factory, furthermore, in revolutionizing woman's way of life, opened the door to limitless social change. For the factory took women wholesale to operate its machines, breaking down their ages-old tradition of seclusion in their homes. The factory confiscated the functions of the home, weakening the family through loss of its economic reason for solidarity.

Most important of all, the factory paid wages to women. For the first time in history, woman has money of her own. Economic independence is probably the chief influencing factor for a majority of the 25 percent of college women revealed by our study who have had the independence, the impatience, and the recklessness to defy tradition and indulge in pre-marital sex intercourse. The fact that few of these college women have reached the status of self-support is immaterial. Consciousness that this world's economy includes jobs for women as well as men must trickle through the shutters of every girl's nursery. It is one of the things she takes for granted.

Deus Ex Machina

Most important of recent inventions, the automobile, has put into young hands an incredible engine of escape. Boys today do not make formal calls on girls, nor pull candy in the kitchen, nor sit in a corner of the living-room and play the game of hearts under the critical eye of young brother. They honk the horn—most of them do not even bother to get out of the car and ring the doorbell—the girl comes running down the steps and they're off and away, out of reach of parental control.

In terms of horse-and-buggy days, every boy and girl in a car is driving the equivalent of 50 to 80 prancing horses at a speed that all the king's horses could never have attained. A youth now has a means of escape from the eyes and ears of inquisitive families. He has a refuge where he is master. He has complete privacy. If the Englishman's home is his castle, so is young America's his automobile. He has taken full advantage of it, not only as a means of going places, but as a place to go where he can take his girl and hold hands, neck, pet, or, if it's that kind of an affair, go the limit.

This facility of escape has been perhaps the most important single element in enabling young people to build a new mode of social life. It is not only the sexual mores which are changing. It is the whole tone and atmosphere in which they key their relationships. Out of the isolation of long trips together has sprung a new camaraderie. The piquant and evasive sentimentality of former days could never have survived these long, close hours of intimacy. Today the relationship is on a matter-of-fact, give-and-take basis of almost complete frankness, but still tingling with the magical lure of youth.

Another recent invention, the moving picture, has been an important influence in breaking down the old sex mores. In every 10-day period the movies now play to audiences equivalent to the total population of the United States. At a moderate price they give the man another place to which he can take his girl. In comparative privacy young couples happily hold hands while the canned product of Hollywood factories bears them off into an empyrean of super-romantic fantasy. The movies' direct influence on the new sex mores through their preoccupation with the more star-spangled aspects of sex is generally recognized. The crudity of the Hollywood accent on sex becomes tiresome to a sophisticated audience. For young men and girls who have not yet had time to discover the comparative scale of values which life offers, the lush sensuality of these shows, night after night, may be very disturbing. The movies have taken off the bedroom doors for young people and turned life into a French peep-show.

Birth Control

A very radical social phenomenon occurred at exactly the right moment to contribute a decisive influence to the molding of the new sex mores: the spread in knowledge of birth-control methods. Nation-wide polls in 1936 reported majorities in favor of the teaching and practice of birth control of 70 per cent (Gallup poll) and 63 per cent (magazine *Fortune*).

Censorship has concealed the rapid expansion of the distribution of contraceptives. In a small, conservative Eastern college town, the best hotel provides in its men's washroom a slot machine which sells condoms for a quarter. It is no longer necessary to find a drug store. Today gasoline stations, tobacco stores, confectionery, grocery, dry-goods stores and pool rooms are stocking this type of contraceptive and they combine to sell a larger share of the total output than the drug stores. It is estimated that the 15 chief manufacturers in this country produce a *million and a half condoms per day*. The average price, under prevailing conditions of cut-throat competition, is about $12 a gross or $1 per dozen, giving an annual value of sales to consumers of approximately $25,000,000. Total retail sales of all types of contraceptives in the United States are estimated by *Fortune Magazine* to amount to $250,000,000 annually although some authorities estimate the business at half this figure.

Religion

The authority of religion had begun to slip before the war. It has never recovered its former influence in the colleges since the post-war jazz era. Numerous surveys of student opinion confirm the decline of religious influence. A study completed in 1937 was based on records of 3,167 students in 39 colleges. Professor Hartshorne of the Yale Divinity School was chairman of the reporting committee. It found that only about one-third of college students today "are interested in religion or consider it a helpful or vital part of their lives." An elaborate study, *Undergraduates, A Study of Morale* . . . published in 1928, was sponsored by the Institute of Social and Religious Research under the direction of John R. Mott. It was based on four years of research and covered 1,100 interviews in 23 colleges. It bears witness on every page to the concern and the helplessness felt by religious leaders.

A dozen impartial observers, writing of college life during the last decade, comment regretfully on the disappearance of religion as a moral influence. James A. Hawes, for 20 years travel-

ing secretary of the D. K. E. fraternity, and, from a different point of view, Dr. E. M. Lloyd-Jones, formerly of the Personnel Department of Northwestern University, an institution with a strong Methodist tradition, have both observed that religion is no longer an important influence in student life. Within the past year several college administrations have been encouraged by what seemed to them a resurgence of interest in religion. The Oxford Movement has made some headway on campuses here and there. Still our study shows that comparatively few students are consciously influenced in their behavior by religious beliefs. Of the 470 men undergraduates who filled out questionnaires, only 6 per cent considered that religion had influenced their code of conduct. In contrast to woman's strongly religious bent in the past, it is significant that only 10 per cent of today's young women acknowledge religious influences in their lives. This is but little larger than the men's percentage.

War

The World War did more than hasten the decline of religion. Those patriotic conservatives who lent themselves most intensely to war activities were the ones, ironically enough, most agonized by the war's carnage of cherished traditions. With the ruthlessness of the obscene war monsters of a Raemaker's cartoon, War reached out a slimy arm and for the time being fairly disemboweled the established sex mores of polite society.

War has always had an intimate backdoor relationship to sex. In the past it has meant license for fighting-men blindly seeking release in sadism and brutal perversions. This time it meant all of that, but more besides. This war found the women of the warring countries on the verge of consciousness of their own economic emancipation and all that it might mean to them.

In that spirit of feverish abandon to which a war must necessarily be keyed, thousands of young virgin women sailed overseas to offer themselves as nurses and war workers. Thousands more, detained on this side, desired passionately to make some sacrifice which would enable them to participate in the mass delirium.

Society, bowing to the inevitable, welcomed its war babies and its war brides, married and unmarried, with facetious levity. But the resultant upheaval was one of the numerous problems which the Treaty of Versailles failed to settle. After the war it was unthinkable that these women or their younger sisters should solemnly return to the old traditions which categorically separated good women from bad. The old codes oversimplified the situation. They had no grays or lavenders. Flattering assumptions about woman's being of finer stuff than man, guardians of our morality, gradually ceased to flatter. Young women were not interested.

Freud

It was in this bewildered, rebellious post-war world that the teachings of Dr. Sigmund Freud sprang into sudden popularity. Freud's technical terms have long since become household words—complexes, inhibitions, infantilism, ambivalence, and many others. His influence has altered the ideals and conduct of many thousands, and was very evident in the students' questionnaires. Many of them referred to his books and many

more quoted his theories and used his terminology.

The College Scene

Fantastic gossip about the excesses of young people during the 1920s still spreads a smoke screen, blotting out realistic appraisal of today's young men and women. Vastly toned down from the hectic post-war decade, current reports still give no indications of a return to the pre-war age of innocence. Rapid changes of the campus patois suggest the fluidity of campus mores. The terms necking and petting are already obsolete in a few colleges. The custom signified persists, however, on every campus and under many new names. To the morose moralist, the variety and levity of the terms are one more sign of depravity.

The 20's were an unreasoning, postwar debauch. "Oh, we're so darned pitiful!" moaned one of F. Scott Fitzgerald's moppets in *This Side of Paradise,* and, "I'm très old and très bored." The 30's have emerged from the depression in quite a different spirit. There is more general drinking but less drunkenness. They are finding out for themselves but they are more deliberate than impulsive.

There is among young people today, says Professor Theodore Newcomb of Bennington College, "less compulsive and more spontaneous demonstration of affection between boys and girls; less soul-struggle on the part of the socially timid, who are freer than before to do as they please; more widespread acceptance, particularly by females, of the 'naturalness' of sex intimacies, with or without coitus; less extreme 'petting' on first or early acquaintance; and more 'steady dating' with fewer inhibitions as to sex intimacy following long acquaintance."

Today's young people reflect the dark shadows cast by the depression in a greater earnestness. The sudden disappearance of the collegiate mode is symbolic. Overnight the college man banished coonskin overcoats, bell-bottomed trousers, cute mottos on his automobile, all the 'rah-'rah gestures. Men and women students dress with a new sobriety. In the eastern colleges which set the fashions for the Middle West, the girls are dressing with the studied simplicity of the smart set. They wear sport clothes, sweaters and skirts, ankle socks, low-heeled comfortable shoes, no hats. The men have adopted the English fashion of wearing coats and trousers that do not match. Formal wear, on the other hand, is increasingly formal. Tuxedos no longer serve for college dances. On many campuses the men must wear tails and white ties.

The records show the unprecedented popularity of courses in economics and politics. Professors, eternally hopeful in spite of themselves, report a new interest in world affairs. The versatile, well-read student who can find his way around among intellectual *objects d'art* enjoys a new prestige, slightly challenging those former campus big men, the athletes and prom leaders. *Life,* in its 1937 college number, gave a two-page spread to University of Wisconsin's Professor William H. Kiekhofer and his Economics 1 A with an enrollment of 845 students. It captioned the professor "the most popular lecturer" and his class "one of the nation's biggest college courses."

Similarly, the report to the Board of Overseers of Harvard University for 1935–36 showed that the proportion of students concentrating on the social sciences had increased 10 percent during the preceding decade, while the Department of Arts and Letters had fallen off 12 percent. In the five years 1931 to 1936 the Department of Government showed an increase of 7 percent.

Statistical studies of student interests reflect normal offsets to the more serious outlook. Analysis of allocation of leisure time in leading university dailies gave athletics the lead with from a quarter to a third of the total. Bull sessions, radio-listening, drinking, car-driving, and just plain loafing consumed 34 percent of the student's leisure as revealed by another analytical study made in 1934 at the University of Wisconsin. Sex interests proved to be one of the most absorbing single drives, involving 75 percent of all students and 8 percent of all student leisure time. The average student spent a little more than 40 hours a week in leisure pursuits. This was more than he gave to study, attendance at classes, and part-time work, and ran second only to sleep.

. . .

Minding One's Manners

Viewers-with-alarm have said so much about young people's lack of manners that it is entertaining to find a woman in close touch with the present college scene writing a book of manners for college girls called *Co-Ediquette,* which went through six printings in six months. As field representative of a national sorority with chapters in 43 universities, Elizabeth Eldridge, recently a co-ed herself, has visited them all from coast to coast. Her advice is moderate and, once the point of view is accepted, fairly conservative.

It is apparent that the college girls who read Miss Eldridge's book are as anxious to make a good impression on their dates as girls have always been. The broader brush strokes are much the same. When saying good night to a date, do not ask him when you will see him again; "that is still his prerogative."

Other aspects of co-ed life are so different from prewar customs that this might be another continent and another century. Take the matter of good form in drinking, to which several pages are devoted. "If you are a co-ed who wants to drink, it is well to say to yourself that even the people who think it is smart to drink think it is disgusting not to hold their liquor. Few men admire a drunken girl or enjoy taking care of a sick one; so be certain you can stop before you start."

This is good advice, but that it should be necessary is startling to an older generation of college women. Mothers and grandmothers would never have needed the practical hints as to what to do on the dance floor if a drunk breaks (asks for a dance) and your partner lets him have it. "Don't refuse to dance with him if he can stand on his own feet. So long as you do not cross a drunk on the dance floor, he is a harmless though at times unpleasant partner. . . . A girl today has to be as adroit as ever in handling a drunken date and in staying sober herself. . . . Never under any circumstances let him drive the automobile. If he gets into a brawl, let him fight it out alone. If he gets sick or unmanageable, turn him over to his fraternity brothers or friends. And if he gets amorous, don't wander with him alone in the moonlight. . . ."

Miss Eldridge sums up the current college mode with a deft generalization. There are, she says, fads in conventions as well as in clothes. The last six years— since the depression—have made this difference, that—"we smoke with more

abandon and we kiss with more restraint. That doesn't mean that we are better than we used to be. Only that flaming youth has lost its novelty."

This sense of a toning-down in the tempo of college life is everywhere recognized, and especially with regard to the place that sex is coming to occupy. The magazine *Fortune* after an inclusive survey of American colleges in 1936 disposed of three major issues in a short paragraph: "Liquor and sex used to be part of the great triumvirate of campus topics that included religion. Today economics is to the fore as bull-session pabulum, with religion playing a minor rôle. Liquor as a conversational topic is passé. Less flamboyant drinking is the present-day rule; there is no prohibition law to defy, hence one can drink in peace. As for sex, it is of course still with us. But the campus takes it more casually than it did ten years ago. *Sex is no longer news and the fact that it is no longer news is news.*"

Thrill-seeking

Dating has elbowed out formalized courtship. "The usual or intended mode of operation of the formal mores of courtship," says Mr. Willard Waller, a professor of sociology at Barnard College, "is to induct young persons into marriage by a series of progressive commitments. In the solitary peasant community, in the frontier community, among the English middle classes of a few decades back, and in many isolated small communities in present-day America, every step in the courtship process has a customary meaning and constitutes a powerful pressure toward taking the next step. . . .

"The decay of this moral structure," Professor Waller continues, "has made possible the emergency of thrill-seeking and exploitative relationships. A thrill is merely a physiological stimulation and release of tension. . . . Whether we approve or not, courtship practices today allow for a great deal of pure thrill-seeking. Dancing, petting, necking, the automobile, the amusement park, and a whole range of institutions and practices permit or facilitate thrill-seeking behavior. . . . The value judgment which many lay persons and even some trained sociologists pass upon thrill-seeking arises from the organizational mores of the family and from the fact that energy is dissipated . . . which is supposed to do the work of the world, *i.e.,* to get people safely married."

Another word for thrill-seeking is dating, a modern custom that flows from modern social conditions. "For the average student," this same observer points out, "a love-affair which led to immediate marriage would be tragic because of the havoc it would create in his scheme of life. . . . The sexes associate with one another in a peculiar relationship known as 'dating.' Dating is not true courtship, since it is supposed not to eventuate in marriage; it is a sort of dalliance relationship."

ERDMAN PALMORE (b. 1930) is Professor of
Sociology at Duke University. In this comprehensive
analysis of the professional reaction to the first Kinsey
Report, Palmore establishes that, despite reservations,
most experts accepted it as a major contribution.*

Erdman Palmore

Kinsey Received

Since the publishing of the so-called
Kinsey Report in January, 1948, a flood
of articles, books and conferences have
praised or condemned various aspects
of the report. There have been 58 magazine articles, 19 newspaper articles, and
4 books published dealing with the Kinsey
Report, plus 4 conferences which discussed the implications of the report.
These make a total of 124 published
reactions, as listed in the bibliography at
the end of this article.

These reactions have ranged all the
way from extremely favorable to extremely unfavorable. At the favorable extreme
are such statements as these:

The Kinsey Report has done for sex what
Columbus did for geography."[1] and,

. . . a revolutionary scientific classic, ranking
with such pioneer books as Darwin's *Origin of
Species,* Freud's and Copernicus' original
works."[2]

At the unfavorable extreme such reactions as the following were found:

. . . it is an assault on the family as a basic
unit of society, a negation of moral law, and a
celebration of licentiousness."[3]

---

[1] Morris, Ernst and David Loth, *American Sexual
Behavior and the Kinsey Report,* 1958.
[2] Albert Deutsch, "Kinsey, the Man and His Project" in *Sex Habits of American Men,* 1948, pp. 1–39.
[3] Francis Sill Wickware, "Report on the Kinsey
Report," *Life,* 25 (August 2, 1948), pp. 86–90.

---

*Erdman Palmore, article originally entitled "Published Reactions to the Kinsey Report," *Social Forces*
(December, 1952), pp. 165–170. Reprinted with the permission of *Social Forces* and the University of North
Carolina Press. Most footnotes omitted.

There should be a law against doing research dealing exclusively with sex."[4]

In view of the large and varied number
of published reactions to the Kinsey
Report, it would seem helpful to clarify
the issues involved, first by analysing
the general reactions of the various
professional groups, and second by
classifying the arguments for and against
various aspects of the Report.

Reactions of the Professions

Sociologists, on the whole, have reacted
favorably, though many have pointed
out weaknesses in the Report. Dr. Burgess
called on sociology for further study of
the "significant" though not "sweeping"
changes in behavior brought out by
Kinsey. Dr. Howard W. Odum, in *Social
Forces*, said that the Kinsey Report is
a "must" for sociologists. Dr. Joseph K.
Folsom, in the *American Sociological
Review*, brought out the implications
which show the importance of the social
and cultural group in determining the
pattern of sexual behavior. However,
Dr. Margaret Mead and others criticised the concentration on the orgasm,
the use of volunteers only, the methods
of interviewing, and the concept of
normality.

Most psychologists reacted unfavorably
to Kinsey's treatment of psychiatrists and
of psychoanalytic theory:

It almost seems as if they [Kinsey and asso-
ciates] feel they are voicing unjustified psychiatric opinions and evaluations and must
accordingly attack and depreciate psychiatrists

on the principle that the best defense is a good
offense.[5]

"Dr. Kinsey's remarks on sublimation
are highly controversial."[6] However, a
majority of psychologists seem to have
reacted favorably to the over-all study.
One psychiatrist said that the report "is
the most important and provocative work
on human behavior that has ever appeared."[7] Another said,

The writer believes that he speaks for the
great majority of psychiatrists in giving un-
qualified approval to the enormous project
of studying statistically the sexual behavior
of human beings.[8]

Lawyers seem to have adopted the
Kinsey figures as "standard ammuni-
tion" in cases involving sex behavior.
Several such cases have already been
reported.

Educators in general seemed to feel
that the Kinsey Report indicated the
need for increased and intensified sex
education. Some educators advocated
earlier marriages, especially encouraging
and subsidizing college marriages, in
order to reduce the tensions and frustrations of students brought out by the
Report. Others warned:

Educators cannot look to the study for
direct guidance, since it disregards aspects
of sex that are vital for young people today.[9]

---

[4] American Social Hygiene Association Conference, "Kinsey Report Criticised from Religious and
Moral Point of View," *New York Times*, April 1,
1948, 50:1.

[5] Robert P. Knight, "Psychiatric Issues in the
Kinsey Report," in Albert Deutsch ed., *Sex Habits
of American Men*, 1948, pp. 57–71.

[6] Burgess and Byxchowski, "Sexual Behavior and
Sublimation as Discussed in Kinsey Report Commented On," *New York Times*, June 6, 1948, 48:2.

[7] American Association for the Advancement of
Science, "Kinsey Report Lauded and Criticized,"
New York Times, Dec. 31, 1949, 26:5.

[8] Leo Crispi, "Are Kinsey's Methods Valid?" in
Albert Deutsch, ed., *Sex Habits of American Men*,
1948, pp. 105–125.

[9] Matsner Sidonie Gruenberg, "Must We Change
Our Methods of Sex Education?" in above, pp. 216–
229.

The reactions of ministers and religious groups were widely varied. Catholics generally condemned the Report. The National Council of Catholic Women branded it as "an insult to the American People" and "a disservice to the nation which can only lead to immorality." Mrs. Clare B. Luce approved this action and stated,

mostly or completely favorable; 31 percent were mostly or completely unfavorable.

Praises and Criticisms

Kinsey's statistical findings were hailed as "highly significant." The incidence

Table 1.   Attitudes Toward the Kinsey Report in the
Published Reactions Analysed in this Article

Reaction	Number	Percent
Completely Favorable	48	38.7
Mostly Favorable	31	25.0
Neutral	6	4.9
Mostly Unfavorable	21	16.9
Completely Unfavorable. . .	18	14.5
Total	124	100.0

The Kinsey Report, like all cheap thrillers, would fall into obscurity if so much attention were not paid it.

Protestant and Jewish groups generally accepted the Report, though some pointed out some of its weaknesses. Dr. Roy Burkhart, in the *Christian Century*, said, "It presents a challenge to the church . . . to be met with a constructive program of guidance."

Penologists stated that Kinsey had "failed utterly to convey the dread enormity of the problem." They said that he had underestimated the sex-stimulants, frustrations, and distortions of sexual behavior in prisons.

The public reacted favorably by a large majority. A Gallup Poll found that five out of six persons with opinions on the Kinsey Survey thought that it was a "good thing."

The majority of the published reactions was favorable, as shown by Table 1, above, 64 percent of the reactions were

statistics, as follows, were most frequently mentioned:

Of American males:
86 percent have pre-marital intercourse by the age of thirty.
37 percent, at some time in their lives, engage in homosexual activity climaxed by orgasm.
70 percent have, at some time, intercourse with prostitutes.
97 percent engage in forms of sexual activity, at some time of their lives, that are punishable as crimes under the law.
Of American married males, 40 percent have been involved in extra-marital relations.
Of American farm boys, 16 percent have sexual contacts with animals.[10]

The frequency and pattern-of-outlet differences between various different social class and age groups were often commented on as "striking."

[10] Alfred C. Kinsey, Wardell B. Pomeroy, and Clyde E. Martin, *Sexual Behavior in the Human Male*, 1948.

Human sex patterns, Kinsey observes, are based on three major factors—the biologic, the psychologic, and the social. Of these, the social factor is the most important. . . . The upper level group tends to view sex from a moral standpoint . . . condemns lower level morality as lacking in the proper ideals and righteousness. The lower level group, on the other hand, regards sexual behavior from the standpoint of the natural and the unnatural. To most members of this group, sexual intercourse seems natural and therefore right whether or not it has legal sanction. They view as disgusting perversions many of the love making habits, such as deep kissing, considered "civilized" by upper level people.

The Kinsey survey reveals that the height of sexual capacity and activity in human males is usually reached in the late teens.

The younger generation is not going to the dogs morally.

In addition to the findings, the statistical methods used were often praised. It was claimed that the Kinsey survey was the first of its kind with such a large number of histories amassed (12,000) and with plans for an ultimately much greater number of histories (100,000). The large number of *different* groups sampled was also praised:

There are hundreds of different groups sampled, based on the twelve outstanding variables among human beings that are likely to be sources of differences in sex habits. These are sex, race-cultural group, marital status, age, age of adolescence, educational level, occupational class of subject, occupational class of parent, rural-urban background, religious group, degree of religious adherence, and geographic origin.

What has been illustrated here in a small way (holding all but one variable constant in a series of groups), Kinsey is doing in a big

way—indeed, in a bigger way than has been attempted before in human experimentation.[11]

On the other hand, the statistical weaknesses received next to the highest number of criticisms. One statistician said,

There are numerous errors in the way the figures add up and are presented. . . . There are also errors in analysing and interpreting the findings. . . . Many of the most startling of Kinsey's conclusions—such as those describing sex differences among social classes—have no statistical base.[12]

It was often pointed out that the sampling was not a proportional representation of the total population. Some groups such as college men are over-represented, whereas many groups such as farmers and Catholics are under-represented and some groups such as Negroes, Southerners, and Westerners are not represented at all. In rebuttal to this criticism, it was pointed out that Kinsey used an "experimental sample" rather than a "representative sample." An "experimental sample" was said to have the advantages of being able to be weighted to give an over-all average which is all a "representative sample" can do, plus being able to give a finer description and distinction of the smaller groups on which it is based.

A second specific statistical criticism was that Kinsey depended entirely on volunteers—

and the exclusive use of volunteers may make the results unrepresentative, giving an undue proportion of those motivated by exhibitionism or an unconscious drive to "tell all."[13]

In rebuttal to this, it was stated that in

---

[11] Leo Crispi, *op. cit.*
[12] W. A. Wallis, "Report on Kinsey," *Science Digest,* 27, (March 1950), p. 72.
[13] Francis Sill Wickware, *op. cit.*

order to secure a valid interview of the intimate type of data covered by this survey, volunteers must be relied upon. Kinsey's defenders further state,

. . . he avoids working with collections of people under circumstances where only a single appeal can be made. Rather, he concentrates on those groups to which he can make repeated appeals, working toward the goal of a 100 percent sample. Where he has volunteers from less than 100 percent groups, he feels he can use them by finding out the properties of the volunteer cases and making proper allowances.[14]

It was further stated that there were comparisons made of the findings in 100 percent samples with those of partial samples and that the results were not "significantly different." It was, however, admitted that these comparisons had been done only with college groups, which might be the reason for "no significant difference," and that these partial samples needed to be further compared and investigated for their representativeness of the entire group.

There was a further statistical criticism to which no rebuttal was made:

. . . two ways of getting large figures are consistently used in the Kinsey Report. These are using the *mean* rather than the median or mode, which always gives, in a skewed curve, a higher figure because of the undue influence of high figures from a few persons; and, using accumulative incidence figures and percentages.[15]

Dr. Robert L. Dickinson praised certain aspects of Kinsey's interviewing techniques. He said in particular that the use of Kinsey's code sheets had several advantages over the other methods usually used. A summary of these advantages is as follows:

Speed, not slowing down the interview as long-hand notation tends to do; continued rapport between the interviewer and interviewee, the interviewer being able to jot down the answer in code, with his eyes hardly leaving the interviewee; accuracy, not being dependent on inaccurate memory during the interview; and, complete confidence of the interviewee in the secrecy of his history since it is taken down in an unbreakable code known only to four persons, and is never translated.

Another aspect of Kinsey's interviewing technique, the use of only a few highly trained interviewers as opposed to the use of an army of interviewers as is done in most public opinion surveys, was praised. It was claimed that a few highly trained interviewers can use a flexible interview utilizing whatever method of approach suited the case best, at the same time being able to recognize invalid answers on the basis of his experience in the field and thus obtain more valid results than the public-opinion type surveyor with his fixed set of questions and approaches.

The weaknesses of Kinsey's interviewing methods were mentioned nearly as often (19 times) as the statistical criticisms (22 times). These are as follows:

1. Memory recall, especially of ages when certain events happened and of frequencies of certain events, is subject to emotional needs for both exaggeration and minimizing.

2. Denial of certain past events through repression is well known and conscious honesty and cooperative answering cannot alter such forgetting.

3. Confusion in retrospect of fact and fantasy is quite likely to cause many subjects to declare that certain events really happened when actually they were only vivid fantasies or even dreams.

4. With few exceptions, events are never recorded in memory in terms of

[14] Leo Crispi, *op. cit.*
[15] Robert P. Knight, *op. cit.*

figures, yet many of the questions put by Kinsey must necessarily be asked in such words as, 'How many times . . . ?'

5. Events are remembered by associations with other events in the context, but after a considerable lapse of time the given events are likely to be lost or distorted by retrospective alterations.

6. The question asked may be objective, but the reason that the question was chosen may be a bias.

In rebuttal, some pointed out that Kinsey used several different checks to try to test the reliability of his data, a summary of which is as follows:

1. Retakes to see if the interviews are consistent over time;

2. Comparison of spouses to see if they agree;

3. Comparison of other sex partners, such as homosexuals, prostitutes, etc., to see if they agree;

4. Comparison of results of one interviewer against those of another interviewer; and

5. Hidden cross-check questions in the interview.

As a result of these checks for validity, Kinsey found that some of his data seemed highly accurate and other aspects of his data were not so accurate. The following types of data declined in accuracy in the following order:

1. Incidence figures (apparently highly accurate)

2. Vital statistics (age, occupation, etc.)

3. Frequency figures (rate of outlet, etc.)

4. First knowledge of sex phenomenon (least accurate).

Another rebuttal to the above criticisms was that they represent only minor inaccuracies and do not affect the validity of the over-all picture.

Kinsey's 95 percent may be only 91 percent. He may not have equally good samples for all the groups he deals with.

He may be criticised on this point or that. But all such criticism together, even if they were all justified, would still leave practically unchanged the broader picture he presents—would still leave his major conclusions unchallenged.

Some even accused Kinsey's critics of ulterior motives for their criticisms of his statistics.

Too much of that criticism represents an indirect attempt to argue away the uncomfortable revelations made by this careful investigation.

They fall upon the statistics as unrepresentative of the whole population, but it is plain that what they resent is the statistical method.

Several of Kinsey's defenders granted that there were weaknesses in the present report, but pointed out that it was only a preliminary installment of a much larger, more extensive, and (supposedly) more accurate project. The critics then stated that the title is misleading and should be more modest such as "What 5,300 North American White Males Told Me"; that there should be at least some subtitle to qualify the all-embracing title of "Sexual Behavior in the Human Male."

The second highest number of criticisms were of Kinsey's concentration on the orgasm to the exclusion of other meaningful factors.

Kinsey has translated sex into an impersonal, meaningless act, . . . omitted the most important aspect of sexual patterns, its emotional meaning. . . . This puritanical attitude is extraordinarily destructive of interpsychic and interpersonal relationships.[16]

In rebuttal, Kinsey and his defenders maintained that the Report is only a

---

[16] J. Eisenbud and Margaret Mead, "Kinsey Report Scored from Social and Psychological Point of View," *New York Times*, March 31, 1948, 27:5.

preliminary survey of the field, that it already includes "five times as much material on sexual behavior as any previous study," and that he could not possibly have gone into the various psychological and sociological ramifications of sexual behavior. However, some pointed out that Kinsey could have either left out some of his other questions or extended his interviews in order to include some of the psychological and sociological implications, without which much of his ponderous statistics are somewhat meaningless.

Kinsey's normality concepts tied for the second most frequent criticism. It seems that Kinsey confuses, at least in the reader's mind, the distinctions between "normal" in the sense of "prevalent," "natural" in the sense of "existing in lower animal forms," and "normal" or "natural" in the sense of "beneficial" or at least "acceptable."

Effects of the Report

A large number felt that the Report should not have been given such wide distribution:

Popular distribution of survey reports makes it possible for adolescents to believe that what they have previously been told was abominable is actually respectable.[17]

In rebuttal to this, it was said:

It will not put bad ideas in heads nor have much effect on the behavior of its readers.[18]

"If everybody is doing it, I can" is an admittedly possible reaction of the immature to the Kinsey Report. But do the critics of the Report believe such an attitude has not existed? Or that it could have been blocked?

Only an almost sublime arrogance would dare set itself up as the censor of what is fit for the people to know. In a study made of 554 sociology students, it was found that although four-fifths of the students knew what the Kinsey Report was, only one-fifth said it had changed any of their ideas or attitudes, and only 3.3 percent of the women and 6.2 percent of the men said it had changed their conduct any.

The most frequent favorable reaction of all was for changing many of our attitudes and laws regarding sexual behavior.

The time is ripe for the end of the era of hush and pretend.

The Kinsey survey shows how hypocritical and self-righteous the American people are.

Kinsey's findings show that 95 percent of the male population engage with some regularity, or have done so, in sexual practices that are at the same time criminal offenses. If this is true, something is radically wrong somewhere.

In conclusion, it is evident that basic revisions are necessary in sex crime legislation.

However, the most frequent unfavorable reaction was against changing our attitudes or laws, or against changing them too fast or too far. Two articles in the *Reader's Digest* which were symposiums of many authorities' and readers' opinions were entirely devoted to discussing why we should not "change our sex standards." However, a large part of such reactions was against changing our attitudes too rapidly or to too great an extent, whereas most advocates of change seemed to be proposing change of only our most unrealistic attitudes and laws.

[17] *Reader's Digest*, "Must We Change Our Sex Standards?" 52 (June 1948), pp. 1–6.

[18] J. B. Wheelright, *San Francisco Chronicle*, Jan. 1948, p. 25.

Table 2.   Frequencies of Favorable and Unfavorable Reactions to Various
Aspects of the Kinsey Report

Aspects	Favorable Reactions	Unfavorable Reactions	Balance of Reactions	Total Reactions
Changing Attitudes and Laws. . .	41	27	+14	68
General Distribution	17	22	− 5	39
Interviewing Methods	17	19	− 2	36
Normality Concepts	9	24	−15	33
Statistical Methods.	10	22	−12	32
Concentration on Orgasm	6	24	−18	30
Title	2	7	− 5	9
Discussion of Psychiatry.	2	6	− 4	8

Table 2 summarizes the number of favorable and unfavorable reactions to various aspects of the Kinsey Report.

To summarize, the vast majority of the published reactions to the Kinsey Report seem to agree that it is an important work, perhaps the best of its kind that has yet been attempted, but a work with many weaknesses which is only a start toward exploring what Albert Deutsch calls "that last great area of mystery—the mystery of human sex behavior."

Professor of Literature and Criticism at
Columbia University, LIONEL TRILLING (b. 1905)
is one of the most distinguished men of letters in
America. This classic essay makes the strongest case
possible against the Kinsey report.*

Lionel Trilling

Kinsey Denied

By virtue of its intrinsic nature and also because of its dramatic reception, the Kinsey Report,[1] as it has come to be called, is an event of great importance in our culture. It is an event which is significant in two separate ways, as symptom and as therapy. The therapy lies in the large permissive effect the Report is likely to have, the long way it goes toward establishing the *community* of sexuality. The symptomatic significance lies in the fact that the Report was felt to be needed at all, that the community of sexuality requires now to be established in explicit quantitative terms. Nothing shows more clearly the extent to which modern society has atomized itself than the isolation in sexual ignorance which exists among us. We have censored the folk knowledge of the most primal things and have systematically dried up the social affections which might naturally seek to enlighten and release. Many cultures, the most primitive and the most complex, have entertained sexual fears of an irrational sort, but probably our culture is unique in strictly isolating the individual in the fears that society has devised. Now, having become somewhat aware of what we have perpetrated at great cost and with little gain, we must assure ourselves by statistical science that the solitude is

---

[1] *Sexual Behavior in the Human Male,* by Alfred C. Kinsey, Wardell B. Pomeroy, and Clyde E. Martin. Philadelphia: Saunders, 1948.

---

imaginary. The Report will surprise one part of the population with some facts and another part with other facts, but really all that it says to society as a whole is that there is an almost universal involvement in the sexual life and therefore much variety of conduct. This was taken for granted in any comedy that Aristophanes put on the stage.

There is a further diagnostic significance to be found in the fact that our society makes this effort of self-enlightenment through the agency of science. Sexual conduct is inextricably involved with morality, and hitherto it has been dealt with by those representatives of our cultural imagination which are, by their nature and tradition, committed to morality—it has been dealt with by religion, social philosophy, and literature. But now science seems to be the only one of our institutions which has the authority to speak decisively on the matter. Nothing in the Report is more suggestive in a large cultural way than the insistent claims it makes for its strictly scientific nature, its pledge of indifference to all questions of morality at the same time that it patently intends a moral effect. Nor will any science do for the job—it must be a science as simple and materialistic as the subject can possibly permit. It must be a science of statistics and not of ideas. The way for the Report was prepared by Freud, but Freud, in all the years of his activity, never had the currency or authority with the public that the Report has achieved in a matter of weeks.

The scientific nature of the Report must be taken in conjunction with the manner of its publication. The Report says of itself that it is only a "preliminary survey," a work intended to be the first step in a larger research; that it is nothing more than an "accumulation of scientific fact," a collection of "objective data," a

"report on what people do, which raises no question of what they should do," and it is fitted out with a full complement of charts, tables, and discussions of scientific method. A work conceived and executed in this way is usually presented only to an audience of professional scientists; and the publishers of the Report, a medical house, pay their ritual respects to the old tradition which held that not all medical or quasi-medical knowledge was to be made easily available to the general lay reader, or at least not until it had been subjected to professional debate; they tell us in a foreword for what limited professional audience the book was primarily intended—physicians, biologists, and social scientists and "teachers, social workers, personnel officers, law enforcement groups, and others concerned with the direction of human behavior." And yet the book has been so successfully publicized that for many weeks it was a national best seller.

This way of bringing out a technical work of science is a cultural phenomenon that ought not to pass without some question. The public which receives this technical report, this merely preliminary survey, this accumulation of data, has never, even on its upper educational levels, been properly instructed in the most elementary principles of scientific thought. With this public, science is authority. It has been trained to accept heedlessly "what science says," which it conceives to be a unitary utterance. To this public nothing is more valuable, more precisely "scientific," and more finally convincing than raw data without conclusions; no disclaimer of conclusiveness can mean anything to it—it has learned that the disclaimer is simply the hallmark of the scientific attitude, science's way of saying "thy unworthy servant."

So that if the Report were really, as

it claims to be, only an accumulation of objective data, there would be some question of the cultural wisdom of dropping it in a lump on the general public. But in point of fact it is full of assumption and conclusion; it makes very positive statements on highly debatable matters and it editorializes very freely. This preliminary survey gives some very conclusive suggestions to a public that is quick to obey what science says, no matter how contradictory science may be, which is most contradictory indeed. This is the public that, on scientific advice, ate spinach in one generation and avoided it in the next, that in one decade trained its babies to rigid Watsonian schedules and believed that affection corrupted the infant character, only to learn in the next decade that rigid discipline was harmful and that cuddling was as scientific as induction.

Then there is the question of whether the Report does not do harm by encouraging people in their commitment to mechanical attitudes toward life. The tendency to divorce sex from the other manifestations of life is already a strong one. This truly absorbing study of sex in charts and tables, in data and quantities, may have the effect of strengthening the tendency still more with people who are by no means trained to invert the process of abstraction and to put the fact back into the general life from which it has been taken. And the likely mechanical implications of a statistical study are in this case supported by certain fully formulated attitudes which the authors strongly hold despite their protestations that they are scientific to the point of holding no attitudes whatever.

These, I believe, are valid objections to the book's indiscriminate circulation. And yet I also believe that there is something good about the manner of publication, something honest and right. Every complex society has its agencies which are "concerned with the direction of human behavior," but we today are developing a new element in that old activity, the element of scientific knowledge. Whatever the Report claims for itself, the social sciences in general no longer pretend that they can merely describe what people do; they now have the clear consciousness of their power to manipulate and adjust. First for industry and then for government, sociology has shown its instrumental nature. A government which makes use of social knowledge still suggests benignity; and in an age that daily brings the proliferation of government by police methods it may suggest the very spirit of rational liberalism. Yet at least one sociologist has expressed the fear that sociology may become the instrument of a bland tyranny—it is the same fear that Dostoevski gave immortal expression to in "The Grand Inquisitor." And indeed there is something repulsive in the idea of men being studied for their own good. The paradigm of what repels us is to be found in the common situation of the child who is *understood* by its parents, hemmed in, anticipated and lovingly circumscribed, thoroughly taped, finding it easier and easier to conform internally and in the future to the parents' own interpretation of the external acts of the past, and so, yielding to understanding as never to coercion, does not develop the mystery and wildness of spirit which it is still our grace to believe is the mark of full humanness. The act of understanding becomes an act of control.

If, then, we are to live under the aspect of sociology, let us at least all be sociologists together—let us broadcast what every sociologist knows, and let us all have a share in observing one another, including the sociologists. The general indiscriminate publication of the Report makes sociology a little less the study of many men by a few men and a little more man's study of himself. There is something right in turning loose the Report on the American public—it turns the American public loose on the Report. It is right that the Report should be sold in stores that never before sold books and bought by people who never before bought books, and passed from hand to hand and talked about and also snickered at and giggled over and generally submitted to humor: American popular culture has surely been made the richer by the Report's gift of a new folk hero—he already is clearly the hero of the Report—the "scholarly and skilled lawyer" who for thirty years has had an orgasmic frequency of thirty times a week.

As for the objection to the involvement of sex with science, it may be said that if science, through the Report, serves in any way to free the physical and even the "mechanical" aspects of sex, it may by that much have acted to free the emotions it might seem to deny. And perhaps only science could effectively undertake the task of freeing sexuality from science itself. Nothing so much as science has reinforced the moralistic or religious prohibitions in regard to sexuality. At some point in the history of Europe, some time in the Reformation, masturbation ceased to be thought of as merely a sexual sin which could be dealt with like any other sexual sin, and, perhaps by analogy with the venereal diseases with which the sexual mind of Europe was obsessed, came to be thought of as the specific cause of mental and physical disease, of madness and decay. The prudery of Victorian England went forward with scientific hygiene; and both in Europe and in America the sexual mind was haunted by the idea of *degeneration*, apparently by analogy with the

second law of thermodynamics—here is enlightened liberal opinion in 1896: "The effects of venereal disease have been treated at length, but the amount of vitality burned out through lust has never been and, perhaps, never can be adequately measured."[2] The very word *sex*, which we now utter so casually, came into use for scientific reasons, to replace *love*, which had once been indiscriminately used but was now to be saved for ideal purposes, and *lust*, which came to seem both too pejorative and too human: *sex* implied scientific neutrality, then vague devaluation, for the word which neutralizes the mind of the observer also neuterizes the men and women who are being observed. Perhaps the Report is the superfetation of neutrality and objectivity which, in the dialectic of culture, was needed before sex could be free of their cold dominion.

Certainly it is a great merit of the Report that it brings to mind the earliest and best commerce between sex and science—the best thing about the Report is the quality that makes us remember Lucretius. The dialectic of culture has its jokes, and *alma Venus* having once been called to preside protectively over science, the situation is now reversed. The Venus of the Report does not, like the Venus of *De Rerum Natura*, shine in the light of the heavenly signs, nor does the earth put forth flowers for her. She is rather fusty and hole-in-the-corner and no doubt it does not help her charm to speak of her in terms of mean frequencies of 3.2. No *putti* attend her: although Dr. Gregg in his Preface refers to sex as the reproductive instinct, there is scarcely any further indication in the book that sex has any connection with

---

[2] Article "Degeneration" in *The Encyclopedia of Social Reform.*

propagation. Yet clearly all things still follow where she leads, and somewhere in the authors' assumptions is buried the genial belief that still without her "nothing comes forth into the shining borders of light, nothing joyous and lovely is made." Her pandemic quality is still here—it is one of the great points of the Report how much of every kind of desire there is, how early it begins, how late it lasts. Her well-known jealousy is not abated, and prodigality is still her characteristic virtue: the Report assures us that those who respond to her earliest continue to do so longest. The Lucretian flocks and herds are here too. Professor Kinsey is a zoologist and he properly keeps us always in mind of our animal kinship, even though he draws some very illogical conclusions from it; and those who are honest will have to admit that their old repulsion by the idea of human-animal contacts is somewhat abated by the chapter on this subject, which is, oddly, the only chapter in the book which hints that sex may be touched with tenderness. This large, recognizing, Lucretian sweep of the Report is the best thing about it and it makes up for much that is deficient and confused in its ideas.

But the Report is something more than a public and symbolic act of cultural revision in which, while the Heavenly Twins brood benignly over the scene in the form of the National Research Council and the Rockefeller Foundation, Professor Kinsey and his coadjutors drag forth into the light all the hidden actualities of sex so that they may lose their dark power and become domesticated among us. It is also an early example of science undertaking to deal head-on with a uniquely difficult matter that has traditionally been involved in valuation and morality. We must ask the question very seriously: how does science conduct itself in such an enterprise?

Certainly it does not conduct itself the way it says it does. I have already suggested that the Report overrates its own objectivity. The authors, who are enthusiastically committed to their method and to their principles, make the mistake of believing that, being scientists, they do not deal in assumptions, preferences, and conclusions. Nothing comes more easily to their pens than the criticism of the subjectivity of earlier writers on sex, yet their own subjectivity is sometimes extreme. In the nature of the enterprise, a degree of subjectivity was inevitable. Intellectual safety would then seem to lie not only in increasing the number of mechanical checks or in more rigorously examining those assumptions which had been brought to conscious formulation, but also in straight-forwardly admitting that subjectivity was bound to appear and inviting the reader to be on the watch for it. This would not have guaranteed an absolute objectivity, but it would have made for a higher degree of relative objectivity. It would have done a thing even more important—it would have taught the readers of the Report something about the scientific processes to which they submit their thought.

The first failure of objectivity occurs in the title of the Report, *Sexual Behavior in the Human Male*. That the behavior which is studied is not that of the human male but only that of certain North American males has no doubt been generally observed and does not need further comment. But the intention of the word *behavior* requires notice. By *behavior* the Report means behavioristic behavior, only that behavior which is physical. "To a large degree the present study has been confined to securing a record of the individual's overt sexual experiences." This limitation is perhaps forced on the authors by considerations of method, because it will yield simpler data and more manageable statistics, but it is also a limitation which suits their notion of human nature and its effect is to be seen throughout the book.

The Report, then, is a study of sexual behavior in so far as it can be quantitatively measured. This is certainly very useful. But, as we might fear, the sexuality that is measured is taken to be the definition of sexuality itself. The authors are certainly not without interest in what they call attitudes, but they believe that attitudes are best shown by "overt sexual experiences." We want to know, of course, what they mean by an experience and we want to know by what principles of evidence they draw their conclusions about attitudes.

We are led to see that their whole conception of a sexual experience is totally comprised by the physical act and that their principles of evidence are entirely quantitative and cannot carry them beyond the conclusion that the more the merrier. Quality is not integral to what they mean by experience. As I have suggested, the Report is partisan with sex, it wants people to have a good sexuality. But by good it means nothing else but frequent. "It seems safe to assume that daily orgasm would be within the capacity of the average male and that the more than daily rates which have been observed for some primate species could be matched by a large portion of the human population if sexual activity were unrestricted." The Report never suggests that a sexual experience is anything but the discharge of specifically sexual tension and therefore seems to conclude that frequency is always the sign of a robust sexuality. Yet masturba-

tion in children may be and often is the expression not of sexuality only but of anxiety. In the same way, adult intercourse may be the expression of anxiety; its frequency may not be so much robust as compulsive.

The Report is by no means unaware of the psychic conditions of sexuality, yet it uses the concept almost always under the influence of its quantitative assumption. In a summary passage . . . it describes the different intensities of orgasm and the various degrees of satisfaction, but disclaims any intention of taking these variations into account in its record of behavior. The Report holds out the hope to respectable males that they might be as frequent in performance as underworld characters if they were as unrestrained as this group. But before the respectable males aspire to this unwonted freedom they had better ascertain in how far the underworld characters are ridden by anxiety and in how far their sexuality is to be correlated with other ways of dealing with anxiety, such as dope, and in how far it is actually enjoyable. The Report's own data suggest that there may be no direct connection between on the one hand lack of restraint and frequency and on the other hand psychic health; they tell us of men in the lower social levels who in their sexual careers have intercourse with many hundreds of girls but who despise their sexual partners and cannot endure relations with the same girl more than once.

But the Report, as we shall see, is most resistant to the possibility of making any connection between the sexual life and the psychic structure. This strongly formulated attitude of the Report is based on the assumption that the whole actuality of sex is anatomical and physiological; the emotions are dealt with very much as if they were a "superstructure." "The subject's awareness of the erotic situation is summed up by this statement that he is 'emotionally' aroused; but the material sources of the emotional disturbance are rarely recognized, either by laymen or scientists, both of whom are inclined to think in terms of passion, or natural drive, or a libido, which partakes of the mystic more than it does of solid anatomy and physiologic function." Now there is of course a clear instrumental advantage in being able to talk about psychic or emotional phenomena in terms of physiology, but to make a disjunction between the two descriptions of the same event, to make the anatomical and physiological description the "source" of the emotional and then to consider it as the more real of the two, is simply to commit not only the Reductive Fallacy but also what William James called the Psychologist's Fallacy. It must bring under suspicion any subsequent generalization which the Report makes about the nature of sexuality.

The empasis on the anatomical and physiological nature of sexuality is connected with the Report's strong reliance on animal behavior as a norm. The italics in the following quotation are mine. *"For those who like the term,* it is clear that there is a sexual drive which cannot be set aside for any large portion of the population, by any sort of social convention. *For those who prefer to think in simpler terms of action and reaction,* it is a picture of an animal who, however civilized or cultured, continues to respond to the constantly present sexual stimuli, albeit with some social and physical restraints." The Report obviously finds the second formulation to be superior to the first, and implies with a touch of irony that those who prefer it are on firmer ground.

Now there are several advantages in keeping in mind our own animal nature and our family connection with the other animals. The advantages are instrumental, moral, and poetic—I use the last word for want of a better to suggest the mere pleasure in finding kinship with some animals. But perhaps no idea is more difficult to use with precision than this one. In the Report it is used to establish a dominating principle of judgment, which is the Natural. As a concept of judgment this is notoriously deceptive and has been belabored for generations, but the Report knows nothing of its dangerous reputation and uses it with the naïvest confidence. And although the Report directs the harshest language toward the idea of the Normal, saying that it has stood in the way of any true scientific knowledge of sex, it is itself by no means averse to letting the idea of the Natural develop quietly into the idea of the Normal. The Report has in mind both a physical normality—as suggested by its belief that under optimal conditions men should be able to achieve the orgasmic frequency of the primates—and a moral normality, the acceptability, on the authority of animal behavior, of certain usually taboo practices.

It is inevitable that the concept of the Natural should haunt any discussion of sex. It is inevitable that it should make trouble, but most of all for a scientific discussion that bars judgments of value. Thus, in order to show that homosexuality is not a neurotic manifestation, as the Freudians say it is, the Report adduces the homosexual behavior of rats. But the argument *de animalibus* must surely stand by its ability to be inverted and extended. Thus, in having lost sexual periodicity, has the human animal lost naturalness? Again, the female mink, as we learn from the Report itself, fiercely resists intercourse and must be actually coerced into submission. Is it she who is unnatural or is her defense of her chastity to be taken as a comment on the females, animal or human, who willingly submit or who merely play at escape? Professor Kinsey is like no one so much as Sir Percival in Malory, who, seeing a lion and a serpent in battle with each other, decided to help the lion, "for he was the more natural beast of the two."

This awkwardness in the handling of ideas is characteristic of the Report. It is ill at ease with any idea that is in the least complex and it often tries to get rid of such an idea in favor of another that has the appearance of not going beyond the statement of physical fact. We see this especially in the handling of certain Freudian ideas. The Report acknowledges its debt to Freud with the generosity of spirit that marks it in other connections and it often makes use of Freudian concepts in a very direct and sensible way. Yet nothing could be clumsier than its handling of Freud's idea of pregenital generalized infantile sexuality. Because the Report can show, what is interesting and significant, that infants are capable of actual orgasm, although without ejaculation, it concludes that infantile sexuality is not generalized but specifically genital. But actually it has long been known, though the fact of orgasm had not been established, that infants can respond erotically to direct genital stimulation, and this knowledge does not contradict the Freudian idea that there is a stage in infant development in which sexuality is generalized throughout the body rather than specifically centered in the genital area; the fact of infant orgasm must be interpreted in conjunction with other and more complex manifestations of infant sexuality.

The Report, we may say, has an extrav-agant fear of all ideas that do not seem to it to be, as it were, immediately dictated by simple physical fact. Another way of saying this is that the Report is resistant to any idea that seems to refer to a specifically human situation. An example is the position it takes on the matter of male potency. The folk feeling, where it is formulated on the question, and certainly where it is formulated by women, holds that male potency is not to be measured, as the Report measures it, merely by frequency, but by the ability to withhold orgasm long enough to bring the woman to climax. This is also the psychoanalytic view, which holds further that the inability to sustain intercourse is the result of unconscious fear or resentment. This view is very strongly resisted by the Report. The denial is based on mammalian behavior—"in many species" (but not in all?) ejaculation follows almost immediately upon intromission; in chimpanzees ejaculation occurs in ten to twenty seconds. The Report therefore concludes that the human male who ejaculates immediately upon intromission "is quite normal [here the word becomes suddenly permissible] among mammals and usual among his own species." Indeed, the Report finds it odd that the term "impotent" should be applied to such rapid responses. "It would be difficult to find another situation in which an individual who was quick and intense in his responses was labeled anything but superior, and that in most instances is exactly what the rapidly ejaculating male probably is, however inconvenient and unfortunate his qualities may be from the standpoint of the wife in the relationship."

But by such reasoning the human male who is quick and intense in his leap to the lifeboat is natural and superior, however inconvenient and unfortunate his speed and intensity may be to the wife he leaves standing on the deck, as is also the man who makes a snap judgment, who bites his dentist's finger, who kicks the child who annoys him, who bolts his—or another's—food, who is incontinent of his feces. Surely the problem of the natural in the human was solved four centuries ago by Rabelais, and in the simplest naturalistic terms; and it is sad to have the issue all confused again by the naïveté of men of science. Rabelais' solution lay in the simple perception of the *natural* ability and tendency of man to grow in the direction of organization and control. The young Gargantua in his natural infancy had all the quick and intense responses just enumerated; had his teachers confused the traits of his natural infancy with those of his natural manhood, he would not have been the more natural but the less; he would have been a monster.

In considering the Report as a major cultural document, we must not underestimate the significance of its petulant protest against the inconvenience to the male of the unjust demand that is made upon him. This protest is tantamount to saying that sexuality is not to be involved in specifically human situations or to be connected with desirable aims that are conceived of in specifically human terms. We may leave out of account any ideal reasons which would lead a man to solve the human situation of the discrepancy—arising from conditions of biology or of culture or of both—between his own orgasmic speed and that of his mate, and we can consider only that it might be hedonistically desirable for him to do so, for advantages presumably accrue to him in the woman's accessibility and responsiveness. Advantages

of this kind, however, are precisely the matters of quality in experience that the Report ignores.

And its attitude on the question of male potency is but one example of the Report's insistence on drawing sexuality apart from the general human context. It is striking how small a role woman plays in *Sexual Behavior in the Human Male*. We learn nothing about the connection of sex and reproduction; the connection, from the sexual point of view, is certainly not constant yet it is of great interest. The pregnancy or possibility of pregnancy of his mate has a considerable effect, sometimes one way, sometimes the other, on the sexual behavior of the male; yet in the index under *Pregnancy* there is but a single entry—*"fear of."* Again, the contraceptive devices which *Pregnancy, fear of,* requires have a notable influence on male sexuality; but the index lists only *Contraception, techniques.* Or again, menstruation has an elaborate mythos which men take very seriously; but the two indexed passages which refer to menstruation give no information about its relation to sexual conduct.

Then too the Report explicitly and stubbornly resists the idea that sexual behavior is involved with the whole of the individual's character. In this it is strangely inconsistent. In the conclusion of its chapter on masturbation, after saying that masturbation does no physical harm and, if there are no conflicts over it, no mental harm, it goes on to raise the question of the effect of adult masturbation on the ultimate personality of the individual. With a certain confusion of cause and effect which we need not dwell on, it says: "It is now clear that masturbation is relied upon by the upper [social] level primarily because it has insufficient outlet through heterosexual coitus. This is, to a degree, an escape from reality, and the effect upon the ultimate personality of the individual is something that needs consideration." The question is of course a real one, yet the Report strenuously refuses to extend the principle of it to any other sexual activity. It summarily rejects the conclusions of psychoanalysis which make the sexual conduct an important clue to, even the crux of, character. It finds the psychoanalytical view unacceptable for two reasons: (1) The psychiatric practitioner misconceives the relation between sexual aberrancy and psychic illness because only those sexually aberrant people who are ill seek out the practitioner, who therefore never learns about the large incidence of mental health among the sexually aberrant. (2) The emotional illness which sends the sexually aberrant person to find psychiatric help is the result of no flaw in the psyche itself that is connected with the aberrancy but is the result only of the fear of social disapproval of his sexual conduct. And the Report instances the many men who are well adjusted socially and who yet break, among them, all the sexual taboos.

The quality of the argument which the Report here advances is as significant as the wrong conclusions it reaches. "It is not possible," the Report says, "to insist that any departure from the sexual mores, or any participation in socially taboo activities, always, or even usually, involves a neurosis or psychosis, for the case histories abundantly demonstrate that most individuals who engage in taboo activities make satisfactory social adjustments." In this context either "neuroses and psychoses" are too loosely used to stand for all psychic maladjustment, or "social adjustment" is too loosely used to stand for emotional peace and

psychic stability. When the Report goes on to cite the "socially and intellectually significant persons," the "successful scientists, educators, physicians," etc., who have among them "accepted the whole range of the so-called abnormalities," we must keep in mind that very intense emotional disturbance, known only to the sufferer, can go along with the efficient discharge of social duties, and that the psychoanalyst could counter with as long a list of distinguished and efficient people who do consult him.

Then, only an interest in attacking straw men could have led the Report to insist that psychoanalysis is wrong in saying that *any* departure from sexual mores, or *any* participation in sexually taboo activities, involves a neurosis or a psychosis, for psychoanalysis holds nothing like this view. It is just at this point that distinctions are needed of a sort which the Report seems not to want to make. For example: the Report comes out in a bold and simple way for the naturalness and normality and therefore for the desirability of mouth-genital contacts in heterosexual love-making. This is a form of sexual expression which is officially taboo enough, yet no psychoanalyst would say that its practice indicated a neurosis or psychosis. But a psychoanalyst would say that a person who disliked or was unable to practice any other form of sexual contact thereby gave evidence of a neurotic strain in his psychic constitution. His social adjustment, in the rather crude terms which the Report conceives of it, might not be impaired, but certainly the chances are that his psychic life would show signs of disturbance, not from the practice itself but from the psychic needs which made him insist on it. It is not the breaking of the taboo but the emotional circumstance of the breaking of the taboo that is significant.

The Report handles in the same over-simplified way and with the same confusing use of absolute concepts the sexual aberrancy which is, I suppose, the most complex and the most important in our cultural life, homosexuality. It rejects the view that homosexuality is innate and that "no modification of it may be expected." But then it goes on also to reject the view that homosexuality provides evidence of a "psychopathic personality." "Psychopathic personality" is a very strong term which perhaps few analysts would wish to use in this connection. Perhaps even the term "neurotic" would be extreme in a discussion which, in the manner of the Report, takes "social adjustment," as indicated by status, to be the limit of its analysis of character. But this does not leave the discussion where the Report seems to want to leave it—at the idea that homosexuality is to be accepted as a form of sexuality like another and that it is as "natural" as heterosexuality, a judgment to which the Report is led in part because of the surprisingly large incidence of homosexuality it finds in the population. Nor does the practice of "an increasing proportion of the most skilled psychiatrists who make no attempt to redirect behavior, but who devote their attention to helping an individual accept himself" imply what the Report seems to want it to, that these psychiatrists have thereby judged homosexuality to be an unexceptionable form of sexuality; it is rather that, in many cases, they are able to effect no change in the psychic disposition and therefore do the sensible and humane next best thing. Their opinion of the etiology of homosexuality as lying in some warp—as our culture judges it—of the psychic structure has not, I believe, changed. And I think that they would say that the condition that produced the homosexuality also produces other character traits on which judgment could be passed. This judgment need by no means be totally adverse; as passed upon individuals it need not be adverse at all; but there can be no doubt that a society in which homosexuality was dominant or even accepted would be different in nature and quality from one in which it was censured.

That the Report refuses to hold this view of homosexuality, or any other view of at least equivalent complexity, leads us to take into account the motives that animate the work, and when we do, we see how very characteristically *American* a document the Report is. In speaking of its motives, I have in mind chiefly its impulse toward acceptance and liberation, its broad and generous desire for others that they be not harshly judged. Much in the Report is to be understood as having been dictated by a recoil from the crude and often brutal rejection which society has made of the persons it calls sexually aberrant. The Report has the intention of habituating its readers to sexuality in all its manifestations; it wants to establish, as it were, a democratic pluralism of sexuality. And this good impulse toward acceptance and liberation is not unique with the Report but very often shows itself in those parts of our intellectual life which are more or less official and institutionalized. It is, for example, far more established in the universities than most of us with our habits of criticism of America, particularly of American universities, will easily admit; and it is to a considerable extent an established attitude with the foundations that support intellectual projects.

That this generosity of mind is much to be admired goes without saying. But when we have given it all the credit it deserves as a sign of something good and enlarging in American life, we cannot help observing that it is often associated with an almost intentional intellectual weakness. It goes with a nearly conscious aversion from making intellectual distinctions, almost as if out of the belief that an intellectual distinction must inevitably lead to a social discrimination or exclusion. We might say that those who most explicitly assert and wish to practice the democratic virtues have taken it as their assumption that all social facts—with the exception of exclusion and economic hardship—must be *accepted,* not merely in the scientific sense but also in the social sense, in the sense, that is, that no judgment must be passed on them, that any conclusion drawn from them which perceives values and consequences will turn out to be "undemocratic."

The Report has it in mind to raise questions about the official restrictive attitudes toward sexual behavior, including those attitudes that are formulated on the statute books of most states. To this end it accumulates facts with the intention of showing that standards of judgment of sexual conduct as they now exist do not have real reference to the actual sexual behavior of the population. So far, so good. But then it goes on to imply that there can be only one standard for the judgment of sexual behavior—that is, sexual behavior as it actually exists; which is to say that sexual behavior is not to be judged at all, except, presumably, in so far as it causes pain to others. (But from its attitude to the "inconvenience" of the "wife in the relationship," we must presume that not all pain is to be reckoned with.) Actually the Report does not stick to its own standard of judgment; it is, as I have shown, sometimes very willing to judge among behaviors. But the preponderant weight of its argument is that a fact is a physical fact, to be considered only in its physical aspect and apart from any idea or ideal that might make it a social fact, as having no ascertainable personal or cultural meaning and no possible consequences—as being, indeed, not available to social interpretation at all. In short, the Report by its primitive conception of the nature of fact quite negates the importance and even the existence of sexuality as a social fact. That is why, although it is possible to say of the Report that it brings light, it is necessary to say of it that it spreads confusion.

FRED BELLIVEAU (b. 1926), is Vice-President of
Little, Brown and Company and managing editor of
its Medical Book Division. LIN RICHTER (b. 1936)
is an editor in the Medical Book Division. Mr.
Belliveau edited both the Masters and Johnson
volumes. The long association both he and Mrs. Richter
had with the two researchers qualified them to write
the interpretation for laymen of *Human Sexual
Inadequacy* from which this is drawn.*

Fred Belliveau and Lin Richter

Accepting Masters and Johnson

Rumors about *Human Sexual Response* multiplied as publication approached, although Little, Brown had made no effort to tell even professionals about it. Newspaper reporters, magazine editors, television and radio commentators, and other publishers called for information. They wanted to know just what was going on in so-called conservative Boston. Magazines wanted to buy serialization rights, to which Little, Brown said no. Paperback publishers wanted to purchase the book for distribution by their companies; again Little, Brown said no. In fact, paperback rights have never been sold. Foreign publishers rushed to buy translation rights, and these were sold so that the book would be available throughout the world. *Human Sexual Response* has been now published in ten languages.

Masters and Johnson were beset by the press in St. Louis. There were such pressures for information on both the authors and the publisher that finally, at Virginia Johnson's suggestion, science writers were invited to Boston in small groups to talk with the authors. Publication had turned into a news story that needed covering. News conferences, which many distinguished science writers from all over the country attended, were held at the Ritz-Carlton Hotel early in April, 1966. Everyone invited to the sessions

83

had been provided with a set of proofs before coming to Boston. The writers had done their homework carefully, and with a good understanding of the book they were able to ask a wide range of important questions and to react in an unbiased and unsensational manner. Masters and Johnson say that journalists have always been extremely fair and helpful to them.

In talking of press conferences, Mrs. Johnson commented, "People from the press are required to deal in a world of reality, and what we were saying made sense to them. They were very receptive." Masters and Johnson feel the responsible news coverage speeded the process of cultural change and put them into perspective as changers of the times and as part of the times. In *Human Sexual Response* they had put together pretty much all that was known about sexual functioning, and the members of the press, with their open attitudes, helped to interpret and to present this information in a way the general public could readily understand.

The sizable first printing of *Human Sexual Response* was sold out three days after publication on April 19, 1966. Even though it was a medical book, it rose quickly to number two position on *The New York Times* non-fiction best-seller list. (One quipster suggested that it was "the cleanest book on the list.") There were still some cries from the intellectual community, along the lines of the Farber attack in *Commentary,* that Masters and Johnson were taking the romance out of lovemaking, and that presentation of their material would lead to a world of sex without privacy, tenderness, or naturalness. Malcolm Muggeridge, for example, declared, "This surely is the apogee of the sexual revolution, the ultimate expression of the cult of the orgasm—the American Dream at last fulfilled."

Many complained that the book was hard to understand and that it was written in turgid prose with convoluted syntax. Reviewing it in the New York *Post,* Max Lerner wrote: "They are committed scientists. Hence perhaps the book's language—oh, the language—which is so severely technical and barbarous as to make Kinsey seem a light essayist."

Most of the public took news of the book, its contents and its methods of study in stride. A new day allowing scientific study of sex was about to begin. This was a far cry from the furor raised by Congressman Louis Heller of Brooklyn when Alfred C. Kinsey's *Sexual Behavior in the Human Female* appeared. At that time Heller wanted the book banned from the mails because he felt Kinsey's group was "hurling the insult of the century against our mothers, wives, daughters, and sisters." This was not the only attack on Kinsey; there were many, and Kinsey had only asked people questions about sex. He hadn't watched them in the act! Times had changed.

There were still many protesters, as Masters and Johnson expected there would be. Mrs. Johnson commented, "It's a wonderful thing to be able to sense well ahead of your time what needs to be done; it's another to try to get everybody to accept you instantly. People have to grow accustomed to new concepts. They have visceral reactions that have nothing to do with their intellectual capacity." A number of physicians and spirited citizens wrote letters canceling their subscriptions to *Time* when that magazine ran a story on Masters and Johnson. One doctor complained about "the indisputable poor taste" of the magazine for printing the story, and another asked to be spared any more of these "Masters-pieces." A father of college students wrote that *Time* had reached "the bottom in the pail of filth."

Many serious thinkers in medicine and the behavioral sciences reacted quickly saying that Masters and Johnson had made original and significant contributions to sexology. Frank A. Beach wrote in *Scientific American:*

Viewed as a series of investigations into the functions of the reproductive system, the work reported in this book can be most meaningfully compared to the pioneering observations and experiments of William Beaumont, Walter B. Cannon and others in connection with the physiology of the digestive system. There are obvious similarities to Beaumont's brilliant discoveries concerning the movement of food through the stomach which were facilitated by the opportunity to obtain samples directly through an opening in the stomach of one of his subjects. The present work is also comparable to Cannon's classic experiment demonstrating that the physical basis of hunger pangs is contraction of the stomach muscles, a demonstration made possible by recording the pressure changes in a small balloon that had been swallowed and then inflated to fill the stomach's interior. Cannon's procedure in comparing his subject's report of hunger pangs with the mechanical record of stomach activity is directly comparable to Masters and Johnson's correlation between their subjects' reports of sexual orgasm.

Almost all the editors of medical periodicals lauded the book and its findings, one going so far as to say that he was sure Masters would be "revered for his scientific guts." Reviewers praised Masters and Johnson for their courage in undertaking the work. The editor of the *Journal of the American Medical Association* commented:

To some sex is the ultimate area of privacy, and hence not appropriate for study and evaluation. No scientific criteria can justify such a conclusion. . . . We may look upon Masters' investigation as a natural and inevitable consequence of changing cultural involvement.

Today, many people sincerely feel that the present atmosphere of frankness and public concern over sexual matters is basically amoral and destructive. Nevertheless, even the most critical should admit that, if we are able to free some individuals from neurotic guilt feelings about sex and if we can utilize scientific research to stabilize even a few apparently unsuccessful marriages, some good had been served. None of these admirable designs is achievable through ignorance.

Another reviewer said, "This reviewer in the shadow of Victorian thinking could not imagine a study of sexuality of normal men and women under laboratory conditions." He then went on to say that even so, he recognized the vision and courage of the investigators and the research population: "With certainty the authors have forever disposed of some of the folklore, fantasies and half-truths which have contributed to the pseudo-science of sexuality as evolved in a Victorian society."

Don Jackson, professor of Psychiatry at Stanford University, and a nationally known authority, commented on the opposition to the book from within the medical community:

Many physicians, despite the nature of their profession, are the victims of this culture and are therefore prudes; they resent Masters' investigations as much as if he had taken religion to task. It is not uncommon for physicans to ask: "Is he happily married?" and "What does Mrs. Johnson look like?" But what relevance do these (and similar) questions have to Masters' competence as a medical researcher? Would a colleague inquire how many surgical procedures DeBakey has had performed on himself, or whether he ever suffered from a broken heart?

Even several board members of the Sex Information and Education Council of the United States (SIECUS) voiced reservations about the propriety of the method of the study from psychological, moral, or religious points of view. All agreed, however, that the findings themselves were valuable. (Since publication of *Human Sexual Response,* Masters has been asked to serve as a member of the Board of Directors of SIECUS, and has accepted.) As Harold Lief wrote in *SIECUS Newsletter:*

At any rate, even if the research methods should offend some value systems, the observations recorded by Masters and Johnson have such tremendous potential for the improved medical treatment of sexual inadequacy, for sex education that would lead to mature personalities, and for future research, that this should outweigh any possible affront to some sensibilities.

Colin Hindley, a biologist at the University of London, captured the feeling of the times nicely when he said of the book, "If we are inclined to regard sexual union as something so sacrosanct that it should not be open to investigation, we should remember that a similar view was taken regarding the stars in Galileo's day."

During the years since the publication of *Human Sexual Response* there has been no serious scientific challenge to it. The findings reported in it have become widely accepted. In assessing acceptance with the medical community today, Masters says:

It is inevitably true that medical training engenders a healthy suspicion—and that is good. Findings should be considered wrong until they can be proved right. This takes years. We have passed from the black area in terms of acceptance of *Human Sexual Response* to a gray area, a middle ground. That is the way it should be. I think we are handicapped some because the techniques we originated have been taken and bastardized by a lot of quacks. This still tends to make a certain section on medicine think we are quacks too. Until they read our work in depth they should be skeptical.

Many critics charged that the book was being bought by the public for titillation. If there was some truth in this, it was far from the prime reason. The authors had deliberately tried to take out or change anything in the book that might be misconstrued as pornographic, and, as one Catholic publication aptly commented, "For those seeking pornography, much more stimulating material is available at considerably less cost than the ten dollars for the Masters-Johnson report."

People mostly bought the book for information. This became quickly apparent; just after publication Masters and Johnson began receiving letters which eventually numbered in the thousands. Eighty percent were from people asking for help with sexual problems. Perhaps ten percent were hate letters, the rest praise or encouragement.

Many people also wrote long, unhappy letters to the publisher, ordering the book and detailing, in page after page, their own sexual sufferings. All these letters were sent to Dr. Masters and Mrs. Johnson for replies. They would not diagnose or treat anyone's problem by mail, but tried always to refer the person to a competent counselor near his own home. Sometimes they arranged to have the couple come to St. Louis for treatment. It is difficult to convey to anyone who has never seen these desperate letters the seriousness and enormity of sexual problems in America. Letters to Masters and Johnson imploring them for help even went so far as to offer payment—any amount—for advice. Some not so serious inquiries also came to Little, Brown. A major Hollywood film studio called to buy movie rights to the book. The caller was asked if he had actually read it. He admitted he had not, but said he understood that it was a very good story.

A New York theater agent phoned to inquire if the musical-comedy rights for the book were available. An American pornographer living in Europe wrote lengthy letters begging the publisher to let him handle all of the European rights for *Human Sexual Response*. His plan was to work the book into a series of still photographs and action movies, and he assured Little, Brown that he really knew how to sell books outside of the usual bookselling channels. Needless to say, these and other offers of similar nature were declined.

After publication of *Human Sexual Response* life changed dramatically for Masters and Johnson. They were internationally recognized for the contributions they had made. The book was widely commented on throughout the world. Before publication lecture invitations were frequent, but afterward, the number of requests was all but overwhelming. They went on a series of one-night stands that would have done in the hardiest traveler. They said they could hardly tell where they were without looking at the hotel matches. In 1967 they were away from St. Louis lecturing for four months; in 1968 for four and a half months. "We had to appear in a variety of places and before a variety of disciplines and let people know we didn't have two heads," said Masters. They admit it was a nightmarish grind, and vowed they would never do it again. About the travel Masters commented, "I don't know how much good we did, but I know we neutralized a lot of the bad, and we got an education by going around."

Their reception around the country was usually good, although they did meet hostile audiences from time to time. As a lecture team they are especially effective. Masters handles the medical aspects; Mrs. Johnson, who thinks of herself as a "people person," gets through to individuals of all kinds in every audience, while competently and perceptively explaining the psychologic aspects of the work. They have talked before thousands of people. In looking back, they find it is hard to assess just how much they educated their audiences, whether professional or general. Mrs. Johnson believes, "We made people more comfortable with the subject. I don't think we really educated. You must make sexual material palatable because so many sexual facts are against individual beliefs. Many in the audiences were so busy contending with their own 'visceral clutch' that they didn't really hear a lot of what we said."

Whether the audience was professional or student, the questions people asked were everywhere very much the same. Neither group had accurate information about sexual functioning. In fact, students were apt to be more free about asking questions than were professionals, especially doctors accompanied by their wives. The physicians did not want their wives to be aware of their ignorance and were hesitant to ask questions. Masters and Johnson gradually developed techniques of opening discussions with such groups. One device they employed when speaking before a professional, middle-aged audience was to pose a sample question in a way to divert the attention of people in the audience away from themselves. One of them might say, for example, after asking for questions and getting no response, "Your son, if he is representative of most young people with whom we speak, would want to ask about the size of the penis and whether a larger one would make him a better lover." Or, "Girls your daughter's age frequently ask how often should people have intercourse when they are married." Of course, these are the questions people of all ages want to ask. Often wives would ask the first questions, and the physicians would follow with their own inquiries. Many receptive doctors wanted to know how they could apply the Foundation's findings to their own practices.

Masters and Johnson completed eleven years of work with patients in treatment before writing their second book, *Human Sexual Inadequacy*. Their final statistics could not be gathered and assimilated until late 1969, just a few months before they began writing. The entire book was completed in six weeks, with Masters and Johnson again setting work schedules for themselves that would have exhausted most people. They promised themselves and their publishers, Little, Brown, that they would have their manuscript ready on January 1, 1970, and they did. As Mrs. Johnson said, "Bill has never been known to miss a deadline."

LESLIE H. FARBER (b. 1912) is an author and eminent psychoanalyst who practices privately in Washington, D.C. In this strong if somewhat prejudiced essay he uses the work of Masters and Johnson as a touchstone to explore the cultural resonance of sexuality in modern life.*

Leslie H. Farber

"I'm Sorry, Dear"

And the eyes of them both were opened, and they knew that they were naked; and they sewed fig leaves together, and made themselves aprons.

—Genesis

Lust is more abstract than logic; it seeks (hope triumphing over experience) for some purely sexual, hence purely imaginary, conjunction of an impossible maleness with an impossible femaleness.

—C. S. Lewis[1]

The modern dialogue which furnishes me my title is practiced throughout the Western world. As a theme with only a limited number of variations, it cannot

[1] C. S. Lewis, *The Allegory of Love*. New York: Oxford University Press, 1958, p. 196.

sustain much repetition: familiarity breeds silence; although never really abandoned, the script quickly becomes implicit. When reduced to a dumb show — or perhaps to no more than a monosyllabic token — it still remains faithful to its pathetic premise. However, for the purposes of introduction I shall try to represent its essence in a wholly explicit manner. The man speaks first.

"Did you?"

"Did *you?* You *did,* didn't you?"

"Yes, I'm afraid I—Oh, I'm sorry! I *am* sorry. I know how it makes you feel."

"Oh, don't worry about it. I'm sure I'll quiet down after a while."

*Chapter 3 of *The Ways of the Will* by Leslie H. Farber. © 1966 by Leslie H. Farber, Basic Books, Inc. Publishers, New York.

"I'm *so* sorry, dearest. Let me help you."

"I'd rather you didn't."

"But, I . . ."

"What good is it when you're just— when you don't really want to? You know perfectly well, if you don't *really* want to, it doesn't work."

"But I *do really* want to! I *want* to! Believe me. It *will* work, you'll see. Only let me!"

"Please, couldn't we just forget it? For now the thing is done, finished. Besides, it's not really that important. My tension always wears off eventually. And anyhow—maybe next time it'll be different."

"Oh, it *will*, I *know* it will. Next time I won't be so tired or so eager. I'll make sure of that. Next time it's going to be *fine!* . . . But about tonight—I'm sorry, dear."

Unhappily, no end to talking and trying for our pathetic lovers. To deaden self-consciousness they may turn to alcohol or sedatives, seeking the animal indifference that is unencumbered with hesitations, reservations, grievances—in short, all those human tangles that create the sexual abyss they will themselves to bridge. To delay his moment, to quicken hers, they may try to assist the chemicals by thinking of other matters—football games and cocktail parties—in order finally to arrive at that mutual consummation which, hopefully, will prove their sufficiency unto each other, if not their love. All the strategies and prescriptions of sexology that have often failed them in the past are not cast aside but stubbornly returned to, if only because in such an impasse there is nothing else. Instead of alcohol or drugs or irrelevant reveries they may—in solitude or mutuality—resort to sex itself as their seda-

tive, intending the first try to spend their energies just enough to dull self-consciousness and thicken their passion to the "spontaneity" necessary for their second and final attempt.

Although normally truthful people, our lovers are continually tempted by deception and simulation: he may try to conceal his moment, she to simulate hers—as they stalk their equalitarian ideal. It can happen that they will achieve simultaneity by means of one or several or none of these devices. But their success—in the midst of their congratulations —will be as dispiriting as their failures. For one thing, the joy the lovers sought in this manner will be either absent or too fictitious to be believed. Furthermore, once the moment has subsided they must reckon with the extraordinary efforts that brought it about—efforts that appear too extraordinary for ordinary day-to-day existence. Thus does it happen that success may bring as much as or more pathos than failure. And always lying between them will be the premise borrowed from romanticism: if they *really* loved each other it would work. Small wonder, then, as self-pity and bitterness accumulate, that their musings—if not their actions—turn to adultery: a heightened situation, which promises freedom from the impingements of ordinary sexual life. Or, pushed gradually past heightening, past hope, they may even come to abstinence, which can seem—with some irony—the least dishonorable course.

My conviction is that over the last fifty years sex has for the most part lost its viability as a human experience. I do not mean there is any danger it will cease to be practiced—that it will be put aside like other Victorian bric-a-brac. The hunger will remain, perhaps even increase, and human beings will continue to couple with as much fervor as they can provoke, even as the human possibilities of sex grow ever more elusive. Such couplings will be poultices after the fact: they will further extend the degradation of sex that has resulted from its ever-increasing bondage to the modern will. To those first pioneers at the turn of the century—sexologists, psychoanalysts, political champions of woman's suffrage—"sexual emancipation" seemed a stirring and optimistic cause. Who could have imagined then, as the battle was just beginning, how ironic victory would be: sex was emancipated, true, but emancipated from all of life—except the will—and subsequently exalted as the measure of existence.

At this point I think it only fair that I commit myself, even if briefly, on how sex was, is, or could be a viable human experience. My view is not that of St. Augustine—that man, by reason of the Fall, is necessarily subject to the lust of concupiscence. Nor can I subscribe, at the other extreme, to the position of the Church of England, as reported at the Lambeth Conference in 1958: "The new freedom of sexuality in our time . . . a gate to a new depth and joy in personal relationship between husband and wife."[2] Of the erotic life Martin Buber has remarked that in no other realm are dialogue and monologue so mingled and opposed. I would agree that any attempt to offer a normative description would have to include precisely such mingling and opposition.

Even if we place it optimally within an ongoing domestic world of affection, in which sex bears some relation, however slight, to procreation, our task is still the difficult one of maintaining that sex is both utterly important and utterly trivial. Sex may be a hallowing and renewing experience, but more often it will be distracting, coercive, playful, frivolous, discouraging, dutiful, even boring. On the one hand it tempts man to omnipotence, while on the other it roughly reminds him of his mortality. Over and over again it mocks rationality, only to be mocked in turn at the very instant it insists its domain is solely within the senses. Though it promises the suspension of time, no other event so sharply advises us of the oppressiveness of time. Sex offers itself as an alternative world, but when the act is over and the immodesty of this offering is exposed, it is the sheer worldliness of the world we briefly relinquished and must now re-enter that has to be confronted anew. Residing no longer in the same room that first enclosed us, we now lie in another room with another topography—a room whose surfaces, textures, corners, knobs have an otherness as absolute and formidable as the duties and promises that nag us with their temporal claims. What began as relief from worldly concern ends by returning us to the world with a metaphysical, if unsettling, clarity.

Though sex often seems to be morality's adversary, it more often brings sharply in its wake moral discriminations that previously had not been possible. Because the pleasure of sex is always vulnerable to splitting into *pleasuring* and *being pleasured,* the nature of pleasure itself, as well as the relation between pleasure and power, are called into question. If pleasuring is the overpowering concern, intimations of the actual and immediate experience of slavery or peonage will appear. On the other hand, if being pleasured is most compelling,

<hr />

[2] Dorothea Krook, *Three Traditions of Moral Thought.* Cambridge: Cambridge University Press, 1959, p. 336.

tyranny and oppression will invade experience with some urgency. And finally, should the lovers will equality between these two concerns, in their effort to heal the split, they will personally suffer the problematic character of democratic forms. To some extent our political past influences our sexual negotiations, but in equal measure sexual pleasure itself is a source of political practice and theory.

The list of oppositions and minglings could easily be extended, but such an extension would not change the fact that human sex inevitably partakes of human experience, for better or for worse, and through its claim on the body simultaneously asserts its particular difference, for better or for worse.

Its particular difference from everything else in this life lies in the possibility, which sex offers man, for regaining *his own* body through knowing the body of his loved one. And should he fail that *knowing* and *being known,* should he lapse into all those ways of *knowing about,* which he has proudly learned to confuse with knowing—both bodies will again escape him. Increasingly, as D. H. Lawrence understood, man has become separated from his body, which he yearns to inhabit, such yearning understandably bringing sentimental and scientific prescriptions for the reunion eluding him. Yet it is through the brief reconciliation with his own and his loved one's body that he can now grasp—and endure—the bodily estrangement that has always been his lot, without succumbing to the blandishments that would betray the realities of both sides of his duality.

In order to develop more concretely my conviction that sex for the most part has lost its viability as a human experience, I wish to consider the Sex Research Project, directed by Dr. William H.

Masters at the Washington University School of Medicine. Through the use of women volunteers Dr. Masters is endeavoring "to separate a few basic anatomic and physiologic truths" about "the human female's response" to what he calls "effective sexual stimulation." The subject, he believes, has been hopelessly beclouded by "literary fiction and fantasy," "pseudoscientific essays and pronouncements," and "an unbelievable hodgepodge of conjecture and falsehood." His debt to Kinsey is clear, though qualified. He acknowledges his "complete awe" for Kinsey's "time-consuming efforts," which have made his own research not only "plausible, but possible." On the other hand he finds that the work of his predecessors, including Kinsey, has unfortunately been "the result of individual introspection, expressed personal opinion, or of limited clinical observation"—rather than "a basic science approach to the sexual response cycle."[3] Therefore, he has done what was indeed inevitable: he has moved the whole investigation into the laboratory.

I should make clear that Dr. Masters' project itself interests me far more than his exact findings. This project strikes me as one of those occasional yet remarkable enterprises that, despite its creator's intentions, quite transcends its original and modest scientific boundaries, so that it becomes a vivid allegory of our present dilemma, containing its own image of man—at the same time that it charts a New Jerusalem for our future. Such an enterprise, when constitutive, is apt to be more relevant and revealing than deliberate art. Because no actual artist

---

[3] These and all subsequent quotations, unless otherwise noted, are from Dr. Masters' article, "The Sexual Response Cycle of the Human Female." *Western Journal of Surgery, Obstetrics, and Gynecology,* January–February, 1960.

is involved, it is not particularly rewarding to ask how this matter acquires its
revelatory, even poetic, power. Often
its director merely pursues the prevailing
inclination in his field. Yet the pursuit
is so single-minded, so fanatical and
literal, that part of the power of the enterprise as constitutive symbol must be
credited to the director's unflagging lack
of imagination and his passionate naïveté which stay undeterred by all the
proprieties, traditions, and accumulated
wisdom that would only complicate his
course.

I shall not linger over the anatomical
and physiological detail in Dr. Masters'
reports, except to say it concerns the
changes observed on the various parts
of the bodies of his volunteers as they
approach, accomplish, and depart from
sexual climax. Of all the mechanical,
electrical, and electronic devices at his
command in this research, it is movie-
making that seems to give Dr. Masters
the clearest edge over the subjective
distortions of his predecessors.

Since the integrity of human observation of specific detail varies significantly,
regardless of the observer's training or
good intent, colored motion-picture
photography has been used to record
in absolute detail all phases of the human
sexual response cycle. The movie is a
silent one. Wisely, I think, the director
has omitted a sound track, for the tiny
events of the flesh he wishes to depict
are not audible. Moreover, had there
been sound equipment, all one would
have heard would have been those adven-
titious rustlings of any well-equipped
laboratory, and perhaps the quickened
breathing and gasping of the subjects.

The movie opens quite abruptly with
a middle-distance shot of a naked woman,
standing, her head and lower legs deliberately outside the movie frame. One

arm hangs at her side, the other is
stretched toward her genitals in an Eve-
like posture, except that it is immediately
apparent she is caressing, rather than
covering, her parts. More in the service
of decorum than science, there are no
close-ups of her hand. This opening
scene of a faceless woman silently playing
with herself against a neutral antiseptic
laboratory background quickly sets the
tone for what is to follow. The naked,
yet faceless, body informs us this is a
"human female" we are observing. The
other bodies that will subsequently appear
in the film will also be faceless; the viewer
may momentarily wonder, as cuts are
made from one body to another, if it is
the same body he is looking at, until he
becomes used to distinguishing one body
from another by differences in shape of
breasts, distribution of pubic hair and
the like. At no time do any scientists or
technicians appear; they may be pre-
sumed to be standing fully clothed behind the camera. In any large dramatic
sense, the arm manipulating the body's
private parts furnishes the only real
movement and cinematically asserts,
even when not in view, that it will continue to fondle during the photographing
of more microscopic and glandular
events. Since what is to follow will focus
on relatively small and minute areas
of flesh that ordinarily would not be
cinematic, the first shot of the moving
hand heightens the dramatic effect of
the oozings, engorgements, and contractions this flesh will undergo as climax
approaches.

Following this middle-distance shot
that is extended a bit in time to give the
illusion of mounting excitement, the
camera moves in on the skin of the abdo-
men and back, so that the film can record
the fine rash beginning to appear over
the lower body.

Through the use of cuts, several bodies

exhibit their rashes until the phenomenon is safely established. Now the camera moves to the breasts to portray distension, venous engorgement, and changes in the nipples. As these changes are repeated on a number of breasts, we must remind ourselves that the initial arm or arms are continuing their work, although it is obvious that views of such action must be suspended from time to time to allow for certain close-ups. Up to this point, all that occurs in the movie could take place on that lonely, upright body that appeared in the opening scene. Now, quite suddenly and without preparation, that body is no longer upright but supine, and the scene is a brilliantly lit close-up of the opening of the vagina. At this point, something of an operating-room atmosphere intrudes, largely because a speculum spreads the lips of the vagina apart to permit an unobstructed view of all that will occur during orgasm.

It is obvious from this portion of the movie that the source of vaginal lubrication is of special interest to the project, as evidenced by a series of ingenious shots of the wall of the vagina showing the formation of individual drops of secretion. The movie then proceeds with a rush to the point that has been imminent since the beginning—namely, orgasm— objective orgasm, displayed visually in the contractions around, and the dilations within, the vagina. The film ends, as might be anticipated, with a succession of photographs of other bodies undergoing similar spasms. With some shrewdness, the director has withstood the tempting aesthetic impulse to conclude his movie with a final shot of the upright naked body with both arms now hanging limply down. . .

This movie is often referred to in Dr. Masters' writings and, I am told, has been exhibited at a number of scientific institutes throughout the country. So fond is he of this medium that there seem to be occasions when his scientific prose seeks, however incompletely, to emulate not only the objectivity but the aesthetic brilliance of his movie sequences:

If the bright pink of the excitement phase changes to a brilliant primiparous scarlet-red, or the multiparous burgundy color, a satisfactory plateau phase has been achieved.

There is even a point at which the movie medium itself becomes the inventor: like the accidental solution or the contaminated culture, which have heroic roles in older scientific romances, movie-making allows Dr. Masters to uncover "the vascular flush reaction to effective sexual stimulation," which had not been previously described in the scientific literature.

With the aid of artificially-increased skin surface temperature, such as that necessary for successful motion-picture photography, the wide distribution of this flush becomes quite apparent. . . . With orgasm imminent, this measle-like rash has been observed to spread over the anterior-lateral borders of the thighs, the buttocks and the whole body.

Probably it was this discovery of the "measles-like rash" that inspired a more Pavlovian venture which, if read slowly, will be seen to have quite eerie dimensions:

One observed subject, undergoing electroencephalographic evaluation, had been trained for 4 months to attain orgasm without producing concomitant muscle tension in order to provide significance for her tracing pattern. Yet, this patient repeatedly showed a marked flush phenomenon over the entire body during plateau and orgasm, and during resolution was completely covered with a filmy, fine perspiration.

If movie-making is Dr. Masters' main

laboratory device, "automanipulative technics" constitute his "fundamental investigative approach" to "the sexual response cycle of the human female." His frankness here is to be commended—particularly since some scientists might feel that such automanipulation was inadequate to the verisimilitude necessary for laboratory demonstration. Dr. Masters himself does not discuss the issue, but his obvious preference for this approach over "heterosexual activity" does not appear to be ascribable to decorum. To some degree, I imagine, it was the laboratory procedures and devices—particularly motion picture photography—which determined the approach, automanipulation being clearly more accessible to scientific inspection than coition. But more important, there is evidence that Dr. Masters regards automanipulation to be a more reliable—that is, more predictable—technique than "heterosexual activity" in the pursuit of "the more intense, well-developed, orgasmic response" cycle.

This type of total pelvic reaction is particularly true for an orgasmic phase elicited by manual manipulation, but it also occurs, although less frequently, with coition.[4]

Yet even this approach, so admirably suited to laboratory research, must share part of the blame for Dr. Masters' inability to measure the "clitoral body" during sexual excitement.

The attempts to measure increases in clitoral size objectively have been generally unsatisfactory due to the marked variation in size and positioning of the normal clitoral body, and the multiplicity of automanipu-

---

[4] William H. Masters and Virginia E. Johnson, "The Artificial Vagina: Anatomic, Physiologic, Psychosexual Function," *West. J. Surg., Obst. & Gynec.*, No. 69, May–June 1961, p. 202.

lative techniques employed by the various subjects under observation.

Little is told us about the volunteers in this research. Apparently the project began with prostitutes. But when objections were made that such a profession might not yield the best "normal" sample, subjects were chosen among medical students and medical students' wives who volunteered and were paid a modest fee for their activities. Naturally no studies could be made on those who, for whatever reason, would not volunteer. And presumably quickly eliminated were those young women who offered themselves out of their enthusiastic wish to contribute to science, only to discover they could not sustain their sexual excitement in the setting of the laboratory, the paraphernalia, the cameras, the technicians, the bright lights. And even more quickly eliminated were those women who on initial interview were not sure whether or not they had experienced climax: "Our rule of thumb is if they're not sure about it they probably haven't had it."

Other circumstances surrounding the study can only be guessed at. Like much scientific research, this particular project must have been an orderly affair. It can be assumed that the investigators did not wait on the whim of their volunteers; that is, they were not subject to call day or night whenever the volunteer felt in the mood. No, the women were given regular appointments during the working day when the entire research crew was available. Doubtless, too, the directors of the project considered it scientifically unseemly to encourage sexual titillation in their volunteers—certainly out of the question would have been anything resembling a physical overture. Should suggestive reading matter be required by the research—as it indeed occasionally was—it would have to be offered the volunteers in a spirit of detachment; not even the hint of a smirk could be allowed to disrupt the sobriety of the occasion. On the whole, the erotic basis would have to be provided by the scientific situation itself, in addition to the actual manipulation: that is, the prospect of arriving at the laboratory at 10:00 A.M., disrobing, stretching out on the table, and going to work in a somewhat businesslike manner while being measured and photographed, would have to provide its own peculiar excitement. (Thank you, Miss Brown, see you same time next week. Stop at the cashier's for your fee.) So, back to one's ordinary existence.

If these speculations have any truth, what can be said about the qualities that the ideal subject for such experiments would have? In a general way, her sexuality would have to be autonomous, separate from, and unaffected by her ordinary world. "World" here would have to include not only affection but all those exigencies of human existence that tend to shape our erotic possibilities. Objectively, her sexuality would be mechanically accessible or "on call"—under circumstances which would be, if not intimidating, at least distracting to most bodies. Hers would have to be indifferent to the entire range of experiences, pleasant and unpleasant, whose claim is not only not salacious but makes us forget there is such a thing as sexuality. Her lust would lie to hand, ready to be invoked and consummated, in sickness or in health, in coitus or "automanipulation," in homosexuality or heterosexuality, in exasperation or calm, hesitancy or certainty, playfulness or despair. (This would be the other side of that older, though not unrelated romanticism that just as willfully insisted on soft lights, Brahms, incense, and poetical talk.) In other words, her sexuality would be wholly subject to her will: whenever she determined—or the project determined—that she should have reached a climax, she would willingly begin those gestures that would lead to one. To use the modern idiom, all that would be unavailable to her sexological dexterity would be frigidity. Or, to speak more clearly, all that would be unavailable to her would be a real response to the laboratory situation. Insofar as her sexuality was under her will's dominion, she would resemble those odd creatures on the old television quiz programs—also ideal subjects in their own way—who were led from boarding houses to stand in a hot soundproof isolation booth, and when the fateful question was delivered from the vault, answered correctly and without a tremor how many words there were in *Moby Dick*—answered correctly in a loud clear voice under circumstances in which most of us could not even mumble our name. The popularity of these programs (at least until skullduggery was revealed) suggests the audience looked with envy and/or admiration at this caricature of knowledge—a knowledge equally responsive to its owner's will, regardless of contingency or trapping.

A truly constitutive symbol should embody both an accurate rendering of contemporary life and a clear indication of what life should be. Taking, for the moment, only the ideal contained in my description of the volunteer in these experiments, I would say that she is a latterday Queen of Courtly Love, a veritable Queen Guinevere. For most modern men and women, who grow ever more discouraged by their bodies' stubborn refusal to obey their owners' will, this Lady of the Laboratory has long been the woman of their dreams: men long to channel or claim this creature's prompt and unspecific response for their own specific overtures, while women dream of rivaling her capacity to serve her body's need whenever she so wills.

And what of those self-effacing scientists behind the camera who conceived and guided this research? Do they too reflect who we are and who we would become? We know as little about this research team as we know about the volunteers. How the scientific boundaries were staked out and protected against trespass is not described in the reports. Once again we can only surmise, but that there was difficulty is suggested by a remark Dr. Masters made in one of his lectures—namely, that he preferred to have a woman scientist alongside him in these investigations because she helped to make him or keep him more "objective." I assume he meant that having an actual woman present, fully clad in the white coat of science, reminded him not only of the point of the matter at hand but of the more hazardous life to be lived with women outside the laboratory—of the difference between the ideal and the actual.

It would be a ticklish problem how to maintain the proper detachment to protect the scientists without at the same time inhibiting the volunteers. Here the equipment and rituals of research would help. And very possibly there would be a deliberate effort to eliminate even the ordinary frivolity that sometimes overcomes a surgical team in the midst of the most delicate operations, because frivolity in this sort of research might be only a way station en route to the lubricious. Any falling-away into the most ordinary locker-room talk, in or out of the laboratory, would have to be regarded as a danger signal. I imagine each scientist, with

all the resolution at his command, would remind himself continually it was just an ordinary day's work in the laboratory, no different from the work next door with the diabetic rats. At the end of the day, when his wife asked, "How were things at the lab today?" he would reply, "Oh nothing, just the same old grind." And if she pressed him in a jealous fashion, his justifications might resemble those of a young artist explaining his necessity to sketch nude models. Of course, there would be strict rules forbidding dalliance between scientist and volunteer after hours. But should they happen to run into one another in the cafeteria, each would keep his conversation casual, trying not to allude to those more cataclysmic events of a few hours before. Mindful of his professional integrity, the scientist would have to guard against prideful thoughts that he knew her, if not better, at least more microscopically than those nearest her. Most troublesome of his self-appointed tasks, it seems to me, would be his effort to prevent his research from invading his own ordinary erotic life, particularly if it were worried by the usual frustrations. In this regard he would be indeed heroic to withstand the temptation of comparing his mate's response to those unspecific, yet perfectly formed, consummations of the laboratory.

Again, if these imaginings have any truth, how may we characterize the ideal scientist in research of this immediate order? First of all, he would have to *believe,* far more than the volunteers, in a "basic science" approach to sex. This is not to say that he would consider the practice of sex a possible science, even though his practice might eventually be informed by his scientific theories. But it would have to be an article of faith for him that the visible palpable reactions of the organs themselves, regardless of whatever human or inhuman context they might occur in, would speak a clear unambiguous truth to all who cared to heed. In his hierarchy of beliefs, these reactions would take precedence in every sense. The questions we are apt to ask about human affairs, not excluding lust, ordinarily have to do with appropriateness, affection, etc.—in other words, right or wrong, good or bad, judged in human terms. On the other hand, the ideal sexologist, as he presses his eye to his research, finds another variety of drama —inordinately complicated in its comings and goings, crises and resolutions—with its own requirements of right and wrong, good and bad, all writ very small in terms of "droplets" and "engorgements" and "contractions."

The will of the ideal sexologist seems different from the will of the Lady of the Laboratory, but it may be the opposition is more illusory than actual. The latter wills orgasm through physical manipulation. Certainly the sexologist supports and approves her willing—such sexual promptness being ideal for laboratory study. However, while his approval may be invented by his will, it is by no means the most important expression of his will. As a scientist his will must be given to the systematic inspection of the sexual response of the "human female," literally portrayed. To this end he persists in his gadgetry, always at the expense of any imaginative grasp of the occasion.

His will to be a scientist requires his further commitment to any number of willful enterprises; in the present circumstance he finds it necessary to will his own body to be unresponsive—not merely to the events on the laboratory table but to any fictional construction of these events his imagination might contrive, because imagination, at least in this arena,

is his opponent in his pursuit of science. On the surface his dilemma may seem a familiar one, being comparable to older ascetic ventures, particularly of the Eastern yoga variety. But the sexologist's task is actually more difficult: asceticism is not his goal—the very nature of his enterprise points in an opposite direction. He wishes indifference, which he can invoke at will: it may be the project that demands his not responding, but—as we shall see later—it may be other moments, unofficial and unscientific, which seem to call forth his willed lack of response. The will not to respond and the will to respond are related possibilities of the will. In this sense, the Lady of the Laboratory and the ideal sexologist are collaborators rather than opponents. Of course, I speak in ideal terms—whether these ideals can be achieved is another matter. But if the Lady of the Laboratory is a latter day Queen of Courtly Love, then our ideal sexologist is the modern Sir Galahad, and together—separately or commingled —they rule our dreams of what should be.

Let us remind ourselves that most of us could not hope to qualify for this research —either as volunteers or as scientists. But this does not mean the differences are great between us and them. True, compared to ours, their lives have an oversized quality, and true, they are in the vanguard. But in a real sense our fleshly home is that laboratory. Whatever room we choose for our lovemaking we shall make into our own poor laboratory, and nothing that is observed or undergone in the real laboratory of science is likely to escape us. At this stage, is there any bit of sexology that is not in the public domain, or at least potentially so for those who can read? Whatever detail the scientific will appropriates about sex rapidly becomes an injunction to be imposed on our bodies. But it is not long before these impositions lose their arbitrary and alien character and begin to change our actual experience of our bodies. Unfortunately our vision of the ideal experience tends to be crudely derived from the failure of our bodies to meet these imperatives.

Our residence in the laboratory is recent: really only since the turn of the century has the act of sex been interviewed, witnessed, probed, measured, timed, taped, photographed, judged. Before the age of sexology, objectifications of the sexual act were to be found in pornography and the brothel, both illicit, both pleasurable in purpose, both suggesting the relatively limited manner in which will—given absolute dominion—could be joined to sexual pleasure. However else the Marquis de Sade may be read, he at least offered the most exhaustive inventory yet seen of techniques for exploiting the pleasure of the body's several parts, if one wholeheartedly put one's will to it. As a moralist he seemed to say, Why our particular rules? What if there were no limits? More recently, yet still before sexology, it was possible for shy erotomaniacs, disguised as greengrocers, to visit brothels, there to peek at the antics of the inmates. The bolder ones could join the sport. When the performance reached its final gasp our tradesmen, now satiated, would slink back to the propriety and privacy of their own quarters, convinced their ordinary domestic world was discreetly separate from the world of the peephole which they paid to enter. In fact, or so it seemed, the separateness of these two worlds heightened the erotic possibilities of each. The emancipation which sexology enforced gradually blurred this distinction, making it unclear whether each home had become its own brothel or whether every brothel had become more like home. The truth is that sexology eventually not only blurred

the distinction, but by housing us all in laboratories, made both the brothel and pornography less exciting dwellings for our erotic investigations.

When last we left our pathetic lovers I suggested that as their self-pity and bitterness mounted, they might—in desperation—turn to adultery. Yet even for the person who believes himself to be without scruples, adultery—in fact or fantasy—is difficult to arrange, exhausting to maintain. Requiring, as it does, at least two persons and two wills, this illicit encounter risks the danger of further pathos. But if we heed our laboratory drama carefully, we can see there is another possibility preferable to adultery. According to the lesson of the laboratory there is only one perfect orgasm, if by "perfect" we mean one wholly subject to its owner's will, wholly indifferent to human contingency or context. Clearly, the perfect orgasm is the orgasm achieved on one's own. No other consummation offers such certainty and moreover avoids the messiness that attends most human affairs.

The onanist may choose the partner of his dreams, who very probably will be the Lady of the Laboratory, or he may have his orgasm without any imagined partner. In either case, he is both scientist and experimental subject, science and sex now being nicely joined. In his laboratory room he may now abstract his sexual parts from his whole person, inspect their anatomic particularities, and observe and enjoy the small physiologic events he knows best how to control. True, this solitary experience may leave him empty and ashamed. But as a citizen of his times he will try to counter this discomfort by reminding himself that sexology and psychoanalysis have assured him masturbation is a morally indifferent matter.

As a true modern he tells himself that it is not as good as what two people have, but that does not make it bad. Superstitious people of other ages thought it drove one crazy, but he knows better; he knows that the real threat to *his* sanity is unrelieved sexual tension. In fact—he may decide—were it not for certain neurotic Victorian traces he has not managed to expunge from his psyche, he could treat the matter as any other bodily event and get on with his business. So we must not be too harsh with our pathetic lovers if they take refuge in solitary pleasures—even if they come to prefer them to the frustrations of sexual life together. Nor should we be too surprised if such solitary pleasure becomes the ideal by which all mutual sex is measured—and found wanting.

Let us now turn to the phenomenon being inspected and celebrated in our laboratory—the phenomenon that contributes most of all to our lovers' impasse. Of all the discoveries sexology has made, the female orgasm remains the most imposing in its consequences. De Tocqeville's prediction of life between the sexes in America[5] might not have been so sanguine, could he have anticipated first, the discovery of sexology and psychoanalysis, and second, their discovery of the female orgasm.

In the second half of the nineteenth century Western man began to see nature in a new and utilitarian way as a variety of energies, hitherto unharnessed, which could now be tamed and transformed into industrial servants, which in turn would fashion never-ending progress and prosperity. The health of the machine, powered by steam and electricity, and the sickness of the machine if those energies were misdirected or obstructed, were obsessive considerations of the period. It was entirely appropriate to regard the human body as still another natural object with many of the vicissitudes of the machine: this had always been medicine's privilege. But for the first time the scientists, in their intoxication, could forget the duality previous centuries knew: namely, that the body is both a natural object and not a natural object. And once it was decided the dominant energy of the human machine was sex, the new science of sexology was born. With the suppression of the second half of the dialectic, sexology and psychoanalysis could—with the assistance of the Romantics—claim the erotic life as their exclusive province, removing it from all the traditional disciplines, such as religion, philosophy, literature, which had always concerned themselves with sex as human experience. Qualities such as modesty, privacy, reticence, abstinence, chastity, fidelity, shame—could now be questioned as rather arbitrary matters that interfered with the health of the sexual parts. And in their place came an increasing assortment of objective terms like *ejaculatio praecox*, foreplay, forepleasure, frigidity—all intended to describe, not human experience, but the behavior of the sexual parts. The quite preposterous situation arose in which the patient sought treatment for *ejaculatio praecox*, or impotence, and the healer sought to find out whether he liked his partner.

---

[5] "... I never observed that the women of America consider conjugal authority as an unfortunate usurpation of their rights, or that they thought themselves degraded by submitting to it. It appeared to me, on the contrary, that they attach a sort of pride to the voluntary surrender of their will. ... Though their lot is different, they consider both of them as beings of equal value. ... If I were asked ... to what the singular prosperity and growing strength of that people ought mainly to be attributed, I should reply: To the superiority of their women." Alexis de Tocqueville, *Democracy in America*.

If the Victorians found sex unspeakable for the wrong reasons, the Victorian sexologists found it wrongly speakable. (To what extent Victorian prudery was actually modesty or reticence, I cannot say. It has become habitual for us to regard Victorian lovemaking as an obscenity.) Science is usually democratic, and since sex now belonged to science, whatever facts or assumptions were assembled had immediately to be transmitted to the people, there to invade their daily life. Writing on the Kinsey Report, Lionel Trilling finds—correctly, I believe—a democratic motive for the study:

In speaking of its motives, I have in mind chiefly its impulse toward acceptance and liberation, its broad and generous desire for others that they be not harshly judged. . . . The Report has the intention of habituating its readers to sexuality in all its manifestations; it wants to establish, as it were, a democratic pluralism of sexuality. . . . This generosity of mind . . . goes with a nearly conscious aversion from making intellectual distinctions, almost as if out of the belief that an intellectual distinction must inevitably lead to a social discrimination or exclusion.

If we disregard Kinsey's scientific pretensions, we still must recognize his eminence as arbiter of sexual etiquette. Like the lexicographer who finds his sanction in usage, Kinsey discovers his authority in practice: his democratic message is that we all do—or should do—more or less the same things in bed. And any notion lovers retain from an older tradition that what they have together is private and unique is effectively disproved by his cataloguing of sexual manners, providing they join him in equating behavior with experience. As a fitting disciple of Kinsey, Masters actualizes the "pluralism of sexuality" within the democratic unit of the laboratory and enlarges behavior to include the more minute physiological developments, which, too, should belong to every citizen.

The political clamor for equal rights for woman at the turn of the century could not fail to join with sexology to endow her with an orgasm, equal in every sense to the male orgasm. It was agreed that she was entitled to it just as she was entitled to the vote. Moreover, if she were deprived of such release her perturbation would be as unsettling to her nervous system as similar frustration was thought to be for the man. Equal rights were to be erotically consummated in simultaneous orgasm. On the one hand it was unhealthful for her to be deprived of release and, on the other hand, psychoanalysis decreed that an important sign of her maturity as woman was her ability to achieve it. In other words, without orgasm she was neurotic to begin with or neurotic to end with.

Though simultaneous orgasm seemed to be a necessary consequence of equal rights, the problem remained that in matters of lust more than a decree or amendment was required for such an achievement. True, the sexologists were most generous with instruction, but each citizen has had to discover over and over again the degree to which he is caught in the futile struggle to will what could not be willed—at the same time that he senses the real absurdity of the whole willful enterprise. The lover learns, as his indoctrination progresses, to observe uneasily and even resist his rush of pleasure if it seems he is to be premature. When no amount of resolution can force his pleasure to recede, he learns to suffer his release and then quickly prod himself to an activity his body's exhaustion opposes. In other words, he learns to take his moment in stride, so to speak, omitting the deference these moments usually call forth and then without breaking stride get to his self-appointed and often fatiguing task of tinkering with his mate—always hopeful that his ministrations will have the appearance of affection. While she is not likely to be deceived by such dutiful exercises, she nevertheless wishes for both their sakes that her body at least will be deluded into fulfilling its franchise.

As far as I know, little attention was paid to the female orgasm before the era of sexology. Where did the sexologists find it? Did they discover it or invent it? Or both? I realize it may seem absurd to raise such questions about events as unmistakable as those witnessed in our laboratory, but I cannot believe that previous centuries were not up to our modern delights; nor can I believe it was the censorship imposed by religion which suppressed the supreme importance of the female orgasm. My guess, which is not subject to laboratory proof, is that the female orgasm was always an occasional, though not essential, part of woman's whole sexual experience. I also suspect that it appeared with regularity or predictability only during masturbation, when the more human qualities of her life with her mate were absent. Further, her perturbation was unremarkable and certainly bearable when orgasm did not arrive, for our lovers had not yet been enlightened as to the disturbances resulting from the obstruction or distortion of sexual energies. At this stage her orgasm had not yet been abstracted and isolated from the totality of her pleasures, and enshrined as the meaning and measure of her erotic life. She was content with the mystery and variety of her difference from man, and in fact would not have had it otherwise.

Much that I have said, if we leave aside the erotomanias, which have always been with us, applies to the male of previous centuries. For him, too, the moment of orgasm was not abstracted in its objective form from the whole of his erotic life and then idealized. And he too preferred the mystery of difference, the impact of human contingency, becoming obsessed with the sheer anatomy and mechanics of orgasm only when all else was missing, as in masturbation.

Theological parallelism is a treacherous hobby, especially when we deal with movements flagrantly secular. Nevertheless, the manner in which lovers now pursue their careers as copulating mammals—adopting whatever new refinements sexology devises, covering their faces yet exposing their genitals—may remind us of older heresies which, through chastity or libertinism, have pressed toward similar goals; one heretical cult went so far as to worship the serpent in the Garden of Eden. But the difference between these older heresies and modern science—and there is a large one—must be attributed to the nature of science itself, which—if we accept such evidences as the Lambeth Conference—by means of its claims to objectivity can invade religion and ultimately all of life to a degree denied the older heresies. So, with the abstraction, objectification, and idealization of the female orgasm we have come to the last and perhaps most important clause of the contract that binds our lovers to their laboratory home, there to will the perfection on earth that cannot be willed, there to suffer the pathos that follows all such strivings toward heaven on earth.

In 1967 Congress authorized the creation of an advisory commision to discover the facts about obscenity and pornography and to make recommendations as to how the government could best regulate the traffic in it. President Johnson appointed the commission in 1968, and it reported to President Nixon in 1970. This excerpt summarizes what the commission learned about the effects of explicit sexual materials.*

The Commission on Obscenity and Pornography

The Facts About Pornography

Experimental and survey studies show that exposure to erotic stimuli produces sexual arousal in substantial portions of both males and females. Arousal is dependent on both characteristics of the stimulus and characteristics of the viewer or user.

Recent research casts doubt on the common belief that women are vastly less aroused by erotic stimuli than are men. The supposed lack of female response may well be due to social and cultural inhibitions against reporting such arousal and to the fact that erotic material is generally oriented to a male audience. When viewing erotic stimuli, more women report the physiological sensations that are associated with sexual

arousal than directly report being sexually aroused.

Research also shows that young persons are more likely to be aroused by erotica than are older persons. Persons who are college educated, religiously inactive, and sexually experienced are more likely to report arousal than persons who are less educated, religiously active and sexually inexperienced.

Several studies show that depictions of conventional sexual behavior are generally regarded as more stimulating than depictions of less conventional activity. Heterosexual themes elicit more frequent and stronger arousal responses than depictions of homosexual activity; petting and coitus themes elicit greater

*From *The Report of the Commission on Obscenity and Pornography* (New York: Bantam Books, 1970), pp. 28–32.

arousal than oral sexuality, which in turn elicits more than sadomasochistic themes.

Satiation

The only experimental study on the subject to date found that continued or repeated exposure to erotic stimuli over 15 days resulted in satiation (marked diminution) of sexual arousal and interest in such material. In this experiment, the introduction of novel sex stimuli partially rejuvenated satiated interest, but only briefly. There was also partial recovery of interest after two months of nonexposure.

Effects upon Sexual Behavior

When people are exposed to erotic materials, some persons increase masturbatory or coital behavior, a smaller proportion decrease it, but the majority of persons report no change in these behaviors. Increases in either of these behaviors are short lived and generally disappear within 48 hours. When masturbation follows exposure, it tends to occur among individuals with established masturbatory patterns or among persons with established but unavailable sexual partners. When coital frequencies increase following exposure to sex stimuli, such activation generally occurs among sexually experienced persons with established and available sexual partners. In one study, middle-aged married couples reported increases in both the frequency and variety of coital performance during the 24 hours after the couples viewed erotic films.

In general, established patterns of sexual behavior were found to be very stable and not altered substantially by exposure to erotica. When sexual activity occurred following the viewing or reading of these materials, it constituted a temporary activation of individuals' preexisting patterns of sexual behavior.

Other common consequences of exposure to erotic stimuli are increased frequencies of erotic dreams, sexual fantasy, and conversation about sexual matters. These responses occur among both males and females. Sexual dreaming and fantasy occur as a result of exposure more often among unmarried than married persons, but conversation about sex occurs among both married and unmarried persons. Two studies found that a substantial number of married couples reported more agreeable and enhanced marital communication and an increased willingness to discuss sexual matters with each other after exposure to erotic stimuli.

Attitudinal Responses

Exposure to erotic stimuli appears to have little or no effect on already established attitudinal commitments regarding either sexuality or sexual morality. A series of four studies employing a large array of indicators found practically no significant differences in such attitudes before and after single or repeated exposures to erotica. One study did find that after exposure persons became more tolerant in reference to other persons' sexual activities although their own sexual standards did not change. One study reported that some persons' attitudes toward premarital intercourse became more liberal after exposure, while other persons' attitudes became more conservative, but another study found no changes in this regard.

The overall picture is almost completely a tableau of no significant change.

Several surveys suggest that there is a correlation between experience with erotic materials and general attitudes about sex: Those who have more tolerant or liberal sexual attitudes tend also to have greater experience with sexual materials. Taken together, experimental and survey studies suggest that persons who are more sexually tolerant are also less rejecting of sexual material. Several studies show that after experience with erotic material, persons become less fearful of possible detrimental effects of exposure.

Emotional and Judgmental Responses

Several studies show that persons who are unfamiliar with erotic materials may experience strong and conflicting emotional reactions when first exposed to sexual stimuli. Multiple responses, such as attraction and repulsion to an unfamiliar object, are commonly observed in the research literature on psychosensory stimulation from a variety of nonsexual as well as sexual stimuli. These emotional responses are short-lived and, as with psychosexual stimulation, do not persist long after removal of the stimulus.

Extremely varied responses to erotic stimuli occur in the judgmental realm, as, for example, in the labeling of material as obscene or pornographic. Characteristics of both the viewer and the stimulus influence the response: For any given stimulus, some persons are more likely to judge it "obscene" than are others; and for persons of a given psychological or social type, some erotic themes are more likely to be judged "obscene" than are others. In general, persons who are older, less educated,

religiously active, less experienced with erotic materials, or feel sexually guilty are most likely to judge a given erotic stimulus "obscene." There is some indication that stimuli may have to evoke both positive responses (interesting or stimulating), and negative responses (offensive or unpleasant) before they are judged obscene or pornographic.

Criminal and Delinquent Behavior

Delinquent and nondelinquent youth report generally similar experiences with explicit sexual materials. Exposure to sexual materials is widespread among both groups. The age of first exposure, the kinds of materials to which they are exposed, the amount of their exposure, the circumstances of exposure, and their reactions to erotic stimuli are essentially the same, particularly when family and neighborhood backgrounds are held constant. There is some evidence that peer group pressure accounts for both sexual experience and exposure to erotic materals among youth. A study of a heterogeneous group of young people found that exposure to erotica had no impact upon moral character over and above that of a generally deviant background.

Statistical studies of the relationship between availability of erotic materials and the rates of sex crimes in Denmark indicate that the increased availability of explicit sexual materials has been accompanied by a decrease in the incidence of sexual crime. Analysis of police records of the same types of sex crimes in Copenhagen during the past 12 years revealed that a dramatic decrease in reported sex crimes occurred during this period and that the decrease coincided with changes in Danish law which permitted wider availability of explicit sexual materials. Other research showed that the decrease in reported sexual offenses cannot be attributed to concurrent changes in the social and legal definitions of sex crimes or in public attitudes toward reporting such crimes to the police, or in police reporting procedures.

Statistical studies of the relationship between the availability of erotic material and the rates of sex crimes in the United States presents a more complex picture. During the period in which there has been a marked increase in the availability of erotic materials, some specific rates of arrest for sex crimes have increased (e.g., forcible rape) and others have declined (e.g., overall juvenile rates). For juveniles, the overall rate of arrests for sex crimes decreased even though arrests for nonsexual crimes increased by more than 100%. For adults, arrests for sex offenses increased slightly more than did arrests for nonsex offenses. The conclusion is that, for America, the relationship between the availability of erotica and changes in sex crime rates neither proves nor disproves the possibility that availability of erotica leads to crime, but the massive overall increases in sex crimes that have been alleged do not seem to have occurred.

Available research indicates that sex offenders have had less adolescent experience with erotica than other adults. They do not differ significantly from other adults in relation to adult experience with erotica, in relation to reported arousal or in relation to the likelihood of engaging in sexual behavior during or following exposure. Available evidence suggests that sex offenders' early inexperience with erotic material is a reflection of their more generally deprived sexual environment. The relative absence of experience appears to constitute another indicator of atypical and inadequate sexual socialization.

In sum, empirical research designed to clarify the question has found no evidence to date that exposure to explicit sexual materials plays a significant role in the causation of delinquent or criminal behavior among youth or adults. The Commission cannot conclude that exposure to erotic materials is a factor in the causation of sex crime or sex delinquency.

Professor of Urban Values at New York University
IRVING KRISTOL (b. 1920) is also editor of *The
Public Interest.* Here he makes an ingenious case
against the abolition of moral censorship. But is
pornography really as insidious as Kristol suggests?
And what are the moral consequences of having laws
that are meant to be violated or selectively enforced
as here?*

Irving Kristol

The Case for Censorship

Being frustrated is disagreeable,
but the real disasters in life begin when
you get what you want. For almost a
century now, a great many intelligent,
well-meaning and articulate people—of
a kind generally called liberal or intellectual, or both—have argued eloquently
against any kind of censorship of art
and/or entertainment. And within the
past 10 years, the courts and the legisla-
tures of most Western nations have found
these arguments persuasive—so persuasive that hardly a man is now alive who
clearly remembers what the answers to
these arguments were. Today, in the
United States and other democracies,
censorship has to all intents and purposes
ceased to exist.

Is there a sense of triumphant exhila-
ration in the land? Hardly. There is, on
the contrary, a rapidly growing unease
and disquiet. Somehow, things have not
worked out as they were supposed to, and
many notable civil libertarians have
gone on record as saying this was not
what they meant at all. They wanted
a world in which "Desire Under the
Elms" could be produced, or "Ulysses"
published, without interference by philis-
tine busybodies holding public office.
They have got that, of course; but they
have also got a world in which homosexual rape takes place on the stage, in
which the public flocks during lunch
hours to witness varieties of professional
fornication, in which Times Square has

* From Irving Kristol, article originally entitled "Pornography, Obscenity, and the Case for Censorship,"
The New York Times Magazine (March 28, 1971). © 1971 by the New York Times Company. Reprinted by
permission.

become little more than a hideous market for the sale and distribution of printed filth that panders to all known (and some fanciful) sexual perversions.

But disagreeable as this may be, does it really matter? Might not our unease and disquiet be merely a cultural hangover—a "hangup," as they say? What reason is there to think that anyone was ever corrupted by a book?

This last question, oddly enough, is asked by the very same people who seem convinced that advertisements in magazines or displays of violence on television do indeed have the power to corrupt. It is also asked, incredibly enough and in all sincerity, by people—e.g., university professors and school teachers— whose very lives provide all the answers one could want. After all, if you believe that no one was ever corrupted by a book, you have also to believe that no one was ever improved by a book (or a play or a movie). You have to believe, in other words, that all art is morally trivial and that, consequently, all education is morally irrelevant. No one, not even a university professor, really believes that.

To be sure, it is extremely difficult, as social scientists tell us, to trace the effects of any single book (or play or movie) on an individual reader or any class of readers. But we all know, and social scientists know it too, that the ways in which we use our minds and imaginations do shape our characters and help define us as persons. That those who certainly know this are nevertheless moved to deny it merely indicates how a dogmatic resistance to the idea of censorship can—like most dogmatism—result in a mindless insistence on the absurd.

I have used these harsh terms—"dogmatism" and "mindless"—advisedly. I might also have added "hypocritical." For the plain fact is that none of us is a complete civil libertarian. We all believe that there is some point at which the public authorities ought to step in to limit the "self expression" of an individual or a group, even where this might be seriously intended as a form of artistic expression, and even where the artistic transaction is between consenting adults. A playwright or theatrical director might, in this crazy world of ours, find someone willing to commit suicide on the stage, as called for by the script. We would not allow that—any more than we would permit scenes of real physical torture on the stage, even if the victim were a willing masochist. And I know of no one, no matter how free in spirit, who argues that we ought to permit gladiatorial contests in Yankee Stadium, similar to those once performed in the Colosseum at Rome—even if only consenting adults were involved.

The basic point that emerges is one that Prof. Walter Berns has powerfully argued: no society can be utterly indifferent to the ways its citizens publicly entertain themselves. Bearbaiting and cockfighting are prohibited only in part out of compassion for the suffering animals; the main reason they were abolished was because it was felt that they debased and brutalized the citizenry who flocked to witness such spectacles. And the question we face with regard to pornography and obscenity is whether, now that they have such strong legal protection from the Supreme Court, they can or will brutalize and debase our citizenry. We are, after all, not dealing with one passing incident—one book, or one play, or one movie. We are dealing with a general tendency that is suffusing our entire culture.

I say pornography and obscenity because, though they have different dictionary definitions and are frequently distinguishable as "artistic" genres, they are nevertheless in the end identical in effect. Pornography is not objectionable simply because it arouses sexual desire or lust or prurience in the mind of the reader or spectator; this is a silly Victorian notion. A great many non-pornographic works—including some parts of the Bible—excite sexual desire very successfully. What is distinctive about pornography is that, in the words of D. H. Lawrence, it attempts "to do dirt on [sex] . . . [It is an] insult to a vital human relationship."

In other words, pornography differs from erotic art in that its whole purpose is to treat human beings obscenely, to deprive human beings of their specifically human dimension. That is what obscenity is all about. It is light years removed from any kind of carefree sensuality—there is no continuum between Fielding's "Tom Jones" and the Marquis de Sade's "Justine." These works have quite opposite intentions. To quote Susan Sontag: "What pornographic literature does is precisely to drive a wedge between one's existence as a full human being and one's existence as a sexual being—while in ordinary life a healthy person is one who prevents such a gap from opening up." This definition occurs in an essay *defending* pornography—Miss Sontag is a candid as well as gifted critic—so the definition, which I accept, is neither tendentious nor censorious.

Along these same lines, one can point out—as C. S. Lewis pointed out some years back—that it is no accident that in the history of all literatures obscene words—the so-called "four-letter words" —have always been the vocabulary of farce or vituperation. The reason is clear; they reduce men and women to some of their mere bodily functions—they reduce man to his animal component, and such a reduction is an essential purpose of farce or vituperation.

Similarly, Lewis also suggested that it is not an accident that we have no offhand, colloquial, neutral terms—not in any Western European language at any rate—for our most private parts. The words we do use are either (a) nursery terms, (b) archaisms, (c) scientific terms or (d) a term from the gutter (i.e., a demeaning term). Here I think the genius of language is telling us something important about man. It is telling us that man is an animal with a difference: he has a unique sense of privacy, and a unique capacity for shame when this privacy is violated. Our "private parts" are indeed private, and not merely because convention prescribes it. This particular convention is indigenous to the human race. In practically all primitive tribes, men and women cover their private parts; and in practically all primitive tribes, men and women do not copulate in public.

It may well be that Western society, in the latter half of the 20th century, is experiencing a drastic change in sexual mores and sexual relationships. We have had many such "sexual revolutions" in the past—and the bourgeois family and bourgeois ideas of sexual propriety were themselves established in the course of a revolution against 18th century "licentiousness"—and we shall doubtless have others in the future. It is, however, highly improbable (to put it mildly) that what we are witnessing is the Final Revolution which will make sexual relations utterly unproblematic, permit us to dispense with any kind of ordered relationships between the sexes, and allow us freely to redefine the human condition. And so long as humanity has not reached that utopia, obscenity will remain a problem.

One of the reasons it will remain a problem is that obscenity is not merely about sex, any more than science fiction is about science. Science fiction, as every student of the genre knows, is a peculiar vision of power: what it is really about is politics. And obscenity is a peculiar vision of humanity: what it is really about is ethics and metaphysics.

Imagine a man—a well-known man, much in the public eye—in a hospital ward, dying an agonizing death. He is not in control of his bodily functions, so that his bladder and his bowels empty themselves of their own accord. His consciousness is overwhelmed and extinguished by pain, so that he cannot communicate with us, nor we with him. Now, it would be, technically, the easiest thing in the world to put a television camera in his hospital room and let the whole world witness this spectacle. We don't do it—at least we don't do it as yet—because we regard this as an *obscene* invasion of privacy. And what would make the spectacle obscene is that we would be witnessing the extinguishing of humanity in a human animal.

Incidentally, in the past our humanitarian crusaders against capital punishment understood this point very well. The abolitionist literature goes into great physical detail about what happens to a man when he is hanged or electrocuted or gassed. And their argument was—and is—that what happens is shockingly obscene, and that no civilized society should be responsible for perpetrating such obscenities, particularly since in the nature of the case there must be spectators to ascertain that this horror was indeed being perpetrated in fulfillment of the law.

Sex—like death—is an activity that is both animal and human. There are human sentiments and human ideals involved in this animal activity. But when sex is public, the viewer does not see—cannot see—the sentiments and the ideals. He can only see the animal coupling. And that is why, when men and women make love, as we say, they prefer to be alone—because it is only when you are alone that you can make love, as distinct from merely copulating in an animal and casual way. And that, too, is why those who are voyeurs, if they are not irredeemably sick, also feel ashamed at what they are witnessing. When sex is a public spectacle, a human relationship has been debased into a mere animal connection.

It is also worth noting that this making of sex into an obscenity is not a mutual and equal transaction, but is rather an act of exploitation by one of the partners —the male partner. I do not wish to get into the complicated question as to what, if any, are the essential differences—as distinct from conventional and cultural differences—between male and female. I do not claim to know the answer to that. But I do know—and I take it as a sign which has meaning—that pornography is, and always has been, a man's work; that women rarely write pornography; and that women tend to be indifferent consumers of pornography. My own guess, by way of explanation, is that a woman's sexual experience is ordinarily more suffused with human emotion than is man's, that men are more easily satisfied with autoerotic activities, and that men can therefore more easily take a more "technocratic" view of sex and its pleasures. Perhaps this is not correct. But whatever the explanation, there can be no question that pornography is a form of "sexism," as the Women's Liberation Movement calls it and that the instinct of Women's Lib has been unerring in perceiving that, when pornography is perpetrated, it is perpetrated against them, as part of a conspiracy to deprive them of their full humanity.

But even if all this is granted, it might be said—and doubtless will be said—that I really ought not to be unduly concerned. Free competition in the cultural marketplace—it is argued by people who have never otherwise had a kind word to say for laissez-faire—will automatically dispose of the problem. The present fad for pornography and obscenity, it will be asserted, is just that, a fad. It will spend itself in the course of time; people will get bored with it, will be able to take it or leave it alone in a casual way, in a "mature way," and, in sum, I am being unnecessarily distressed about the whole business. The New York Times, in an editorial, concludes hopefully in this vein.

"In the end . . . the insensate pursuit of the urge to shock, carried from one excess to a more abysmal one, is bound to achieve its own antidote in total boredom. When there is no lower depth to descend to, ennui will erase the problem."

I would like to be able to go along with this line of reasoning, but I cannot. I think it is false, and for two reasons, the first psychological, the second political.

The basic psychological fact about pornography and obscenity is that it appeals to and provokes a kind of sexual regression. The sexual pleasure one gets from pornography and obscenity is autoerotic and infantile; put bluntly, it is a masturbatory exercise of the imagination, when it is not masturbation pure and simple. Now, people who masturbate do not get bored with masturbation, just as sadists don't get bored with sadism, and voyeurs don't get bored with voyeurism.

In other words, infantile sexuality is

not only a permanent temptation for the adolescent or even the adult—it can quite easily become a permanent, self-reinforcing neurosis. It is because of an awareness of this possibility of regression toward the infantile condition, a regression which is always open to us, that all the codes of sexual conduct ever devised by the human race take such a dim view of autoerotic activities and try to discourage autoerotic fantasies. Masturbation is indeed a perfectly natural autoerotic activity, as so many sexologists blandly assure us today. And it is precisely because it is so perfectly natural that it can be so dangerous to the mature or maturing person, if it is not controlled or sublimated in some way. That is the true meaning of Portnoy's complaint. Portnoy, you will recall, grows up to be a man who is incapable of having an adult sexual relationship with a woman; his sexuality remains fixed in an infantile mode, the prison of his autoerotic fantasies. Inevitably, Portnoy comes to think, in a perfectly *infantile* way, that it was all his mother's fault.

It is true that, in our time, some quite brilliant minds have come to the conclusion that a reversion to infantile sexuality is the ultimate mission and secret destiny of the human race. I am thinking in particular of Norman O. Brown, for whose writings I have the deepest respect. One of the reasons I respect them so deeply is that Mr. Brown is a serious thinker who is unafraid to face up to the radical consequences of his radical theories. Thus, Mr. Brown knows and says that for his kind of salvation to be achieved, humanity must annul the civilization it has created—not merely the civilization we have today, but all civilization—so as to be able to make the long descent backwards into animal innocence.

What is at stake is civilization and

humanity, nothing less. The idea that "everything is permitted," as Nietzsche put it, rests on the premise of nihilism and has nihilistic implications. I will not pretend that the case against nihilism and for civilization is an easy one to make. We are here confronting the most fundamental of philosophical questions, on the deepest levels. But that is precisely my point—that the matter of pornography and obscenity is not a trivial one, and that only superficial minds can take a bland and untroubled view of it.

In this connection, I might also point out those who are primarily against censorship on liberal grounds tell us not to take pornography or obscenity seriously, while those who are for pornography and obscenity, on radical grounds, take it very seriously indeed. I believe the radicals—writers like Susan Sontag, Herbert Marcuse, Norman O. Brown, and even Jerry Rubin—are right, and the liberals are wrong. I also believe that those young radicals at Berkeley, some five years ago, who provoked a major confrontation over the public use of obscene words, showed a brilliant political instinct. Once the faculty and administration had capitulated on this issue—saying: "Oh, for God's sake, let's be adult: what difference does it make anyway?"—once they said that, they were bound to lose on every other issue. And once Mark Rudd could publicly ascribe to the president of Columbia a notoriously obscene relationship to his mother, without provoking any kind of reaction, the S.D.S. had already won the day. The occupation of Columbia's buildings merely ratified their victory. Men who show themselves unwilling to defend civilization against nihilism are not going to be either resolute or effective in defending the university against anything.

I am already touching upon a political aspect of pornography when I suggest that it is inherently and purposefully subversive of civilization and its institutions. But there is another and more specifically political aspect, which has to do with the relationship of pornography and/or obscenity to democracy, and especially to the quality of public life on which democratic government ultimately rests.

Though the phrase, "the quality of life," trips easily from so many lips these days, it tends to be one of those clichés with many trivial meanings and no large, serious one. Sometimes it merely refers to such externals as the enjoyment of cleaner air, cleaner water, cleaner streets. At other times it refers to the merely private enjoyment of music, painting or literature. Rarely does it have anything to do with the way the citizen in a democracy views himself—his obligations, his intentions, his ultimate self-definition.

Instead, what I would call the "managerial" conception of democracy is the predominant opinion among political scientists, sociologists and economists, and has, through the untiring efforts of these scholars, become the conventional journalistic opinion as well. The root idea behind this "managerial" conception is that democracy is a "political system" (as they say) which can be adequately defined in terms of—can be fully reduced to—its mechanical arrangements. Democracy is then seen as a set of rules and procedures, and *nothing but* a set of rules and procedures, whereby majority rule and minority rights are reconciled into a state of equilibrium. If everyone follows these rules and procedures, then a democracy is in working order. I think this is a fair description of the democratic idea that currently prevails in academia. One can also fairly say that it is now the liberal idea of democracy par excellence.

I cannot help but feel that there is something ridiculous about being this kind of a democrat, and I must further confess to having a sneaking sympathy for those of our young radicals who also find it ridiculous. The absurdity is the absurdity of idolatry—of taking the symbolic for the real, the means for the end. The purpose of democracy cannot possibly be the endless functioning of its own political machinery. The purpose of any political regime is to achieve some version of the good life and the good society. It is not at all difficult to imagine a perfectly functioning democracy which answers all questions except one—namely, why should anyone of intelligence and spirit care a fig for it?

There is, however, an older idea of democracy—one which was fairly common until about the beginning of this century—for which the conception of the quality of public life is absolutely crucial. This idea starts from the proposition that democracy is a form of self-government, and that if you want it to be a meritorious polity, you have to care about what kind of people govern it. Indeed, it puts the matter more strongly and declares that, if you want self-government, you are only entitled to it if that "self" is worthy of governing. There is no inherent right to self-government if it means that such government is vicious, mean, squalid and debased. Only a dogmatist and a fanatic, an idolater of democratic machinery, could approve of self-government under such conditions.

And because the desirability of self-government depends on the character of the people who govern, the older idea of democracy was very solicitous of the condition of this character. It was solicitous of the individual self, and felt an obligation to educate it into what used to be called "republican virtue." And it was solicitous of that collective self which we call public opinion and which, in a democracy, governs us collectively. Perhaps in some respects it was nervously oversolicitous—that would not be surprising. But the main thing is that it cared, cared not merely about the machinery of democracy but about the quality of life that this machinery might generate.

And because it cared, this older idea of democracy had no problem in principle with pornography and/or obscenity. It censored them—and it did so with a perfect clarity of mind and a perfectly clear conscience. It was not about to permit people capriciously to corrupt themselves. Or, to put it more precisely: in this version of democracy, the people took some care not to let themselves be governed by the more infantile and irrational parts of themselves.

I have, it may be noticed, uttered that dreadful word, "censorship." And I am not about to back away from it. If you think pornography and/or obscenity is a serious problem, you have to be for censorship. I'll go even further and say that if you want to prevent pornography and/or obscenity from becoming a problem, you have to be for censorship. And lest there be any misunderstanding as to what I am saying, I'll put it as bluntly as possible: if you care for the quality of life in our American democracy, then you have to be for censorship.

But can a liberal be for censorship? Unless one assumes that being a liberal *must* mean being indifferent to the quality of American life, then the answer has to be: yes, a liberal can be for censorship—but he ought to favor a liberal form of censorship.

Is that a contradiction in terms? I don't think so. We have no problem in contrasting *repressive* laws governing alcohol and drugs and tobacco with laws *regulating* (i.e., discouraging the sale of) alcohol and drugs and tobacco. Laws encouraging temperance are not the same thing as laws that have as their goal prohibition or abolition. We have not made the smoking of cigarettes a criminal offense. We have, however, and with good liberal conscience, prohibited cigarette advertising on television, and may yet, again with good liberal conscience, prohibit it in newspapers and magazines. The idea of restricting individual freedom, in a liberal way, is not at all unfamiliar to us.

I therefore see no reason why we should not be able to distinguish repressive censorship from liberal censorship of the written and spoken word. In Britain, until a few years ago, you could perform almost any play you wished — but certain plays, judged to be obscene, had to be performed in private theatrical clubs which were deemed to have a "serious" interest in theater. In the U.S., all of us who grew up using public libraries are familiar with the circumstances under which certain books could be circulated only to adults, while still other books had to be read in the library reading room, under the librarian's skeptical eye. In both cases, a small minority that was willing to make a serious effort to see an obscene play or read an obscene book could do so. But the impact of obscenity was circumscribed and the quality of public life was only marginally affected.

I am not saying it is easy in practice to sustain a distinction between liberal and repressive censorship, especially in the public realm of a democracy, where popular opinion is so vulnerable to demagoguery. Moreover, an acceptable system of liberal censorship is likely to be exceedingly difficult to devise in the United States today, because our educated classes, upon whose judgment a liberal censorship

must rest, are so convinced that there is no such thing as a problem of obscenity, or even that there is no such thing as obscenity at all. But, to counterbalance this, there is the further, fortunate truth that the tolerable margin for error is quite large, and single mistakes or single injustices are not all that important.

This possibility, of course, occasions much distress among artists and academics. It is a fact, one that cannot and should not be denied, that any system of censorship is bound, upon occasion, to treat unjustly a particular work of art — to find pornography where there is only gentle eroticism, to find obscenity where none really exists, or to find both where its existence ought to be tolerated because it serves a larger moral purpose. Though most works of art are not obscene, and though most obscenity has nothing to do with art, there are some few works of art that are, at least in part, pornographic and/or obscene. There are also some few works of art that are in the special category of the comic-ironic "bawdy" (Boccaccio, Rabelais). It is such works of art that are likely to suffer at the hands of the censor. That is the price one has to be prepared to pay for censorship — even liberal censorship.

But just how high is this price? If you believe, as so many artists seem to believe today, that art is the only sacrosanct activity in our profane and vulgar world — that any man who designates himself an artist thereby acquires a sacred office — then obviously censorship is an intolerable form of sacrilege. But for those of us who do not subscribe to this religion of art, the costs of censorship do not seem so high at all.

If you look at the history of American or English literature, there is precious little damage you can point to as a consequence of the censorship that prevailed throughout most of that history. Very few works of literature—of real literary merit, I mean—ever were suppressed; and those that were, were not suppressed for long. Nor have I noticed, now that censorship of the written word has to all intents and purposes ceased in this country, that hitherto suppressed or repressed masterpieces are flooding the market. Yes, we can now read "Fanny Hill" and the Marquis de Sade. Or, to be more exact, we can now openly purchase them, since many people were able to read them even though they were publicly banned, which is as it should be under a liberal censorship. So how much have literature and the arts gained from the fact that we can all now buy them over the counter, that, indeed, we are all now encouraged to buy them over the counter? They have not gained much that I can see.

And one might also ask a question that is almost never raised: how much has literature lost from the fact that everything is now permitted? It has lost quite a bit, I should say. In a free market, Gresham's Law can work for books or theater as efficiently as it does for coinage —driving out the good, establishing the debased. The cultural market in the United States today is being pre-empted by dirty books, dirty movies, dirty theater. A pornographic novel has a far better chance of being published today than a non-pornographic one, and quite a few pretty good novels are not being published at all simply because they are not pornographic, and are therefore less likely to sell. Our cultural condition has not improved as a result of the new freedom. American cultural life wasn't much to brag about 20 years ago; today one feels ashamed for it.

Just one last point which I dare not leave untouched. If we start censoring pornography or obscenity, shall we not inevitably end up censoring political opinion? A lot of people seem to think this would be the case—which only shows the power of doctrinaire thinking over reality. We had censorship of pornography and obscenity for 150 years, until almost yesterday, and I am not aware that freedom of opinion in this country was in any way diminished as a consequence of this fact. Fortunately for those of us who are liberal, freedom is not indivisible. If it were, the case for liberalism would be indistinguishable from the case for anarchy; and they are two very different things.

But I must repeat and emphasize: what kind of laws we pass governing pornography and obscenity, what kind of censorship—or, since we are still a Federal nation—what kinds of censorship we institute in our various localities may indeed be difficult matters to cope with; nevertheless the real issue is one of principle. I myself subscribe to a liberal view of the enforcement problem: I think that pornography should be illegal *and* available to anyone who wants it so badly as to make a pretty strenuous effort to get it. We have lived with under-the-counter pornography for centuries now, in a fairly comfortable way. But the issue of principle, of whether it should be over or under the counter, has to be settled before we can reflect on the advantages and disadvantages of alternative modes of censorship. I think the settlement we are living under now, in which obscenity and democracy are regarded as equals, is wrong; I believe it is inherently unstable; I think it will, in the long run, be incompatible with any authentic concern for the quality of life in our democracy.

JOHN CORRY is a reporter for *The New York Times.* In this article he sums up what is known about the American sexual condition. Though written before Masters and Johnson released their large studies, and before the latest wave of discussion about the sexual revolution, little has happened since to alter his general position.*

John Corry

Not a Revolution, More a Way of Life

Americans talk more about sex than they did before, but there is little to indicate that they are actually behaving much differently than they did, say thirty-five years ago. For instance, Dr. Alfred C. Kinsey and his associates, who began collecting their information in 1938, said in 1948 that perhaps 20 per-cent of college girls were not virgins. Subsequent studies indicate that this is still a true figure.

They also indicate that Americans are not experiencing sexual relations at an earlier age than before, that promiscuity is still a high-school, not a college, prob-lem, and that the 1920s, not the 1960s, was the time of the great leap forward in permissive sexual behavior. None-theless, there is sexual change, and it deals with attitudes, not behavior. Change is not the Sexual Freedom League, which sells buttons on college campuses that say: "Go Naked." But it is the Sex Infor-mation and Education Council of the United States, which says that sexuality involves mental health.

Change is also the proposal by the National Association of Independent Schools that its 760 members give priority to sex education, and it is the courses on marriage and the family that are offered in more than seven hundred colleges. It is the lectures to student doctors that are now given in twenty-nine medical schools, and it is the suggestion by the Minnesota Department of Health that pupils in primary grades learn about the function of fathers and mothers in reproduction. At its most thoughtful, this change deals with sexual activity as a part of sexuality and sexuality as an expression of personality. The new sex education, for example, deals with more than the question of where babies come from.

A member of the board of directors of SIECUS, the sex information council, puts it this way: "Sex education in the best sense today means training people emotionally and intellectually to be able to make intelligent and well-informed choices among an array of competing alternatives."

SIECUS was founded in 1964 because, another director said, "It was time to deal with this sex mess." There are forty-one directors at SIECUS, and they are almost all eminent in medical science, education, religion, or marriage counseling.

In a year, SIECUS had 2,819 requests for aid and information. They were from, among other places, 460 schools, 223 colleges, 298 doctors, 156 church organizations, 254 professional groups, and 95 branches of government. SIECUS answered with reprints, letters, discussion guides and outlines for community sex education programs. Yet, its executive director, Dr. Mary S. Calderone, says: "We, none of us, know[s] enough about sex." John H. Gagnon, a senior trustee at the Institute for Sex Research at Indiana University, agrees. He deplores the paucity of research about sexual behavior and says that the "image of sexuality today is one of crisis and change." Perhaps there really is crisis, he says, but he is not so sure about change. "We have just discovered statistics," he says, "and now we are discovering ourselves." He also says that the rules on

speaking about sex have changed and that because Americans talk more about it they conclude that there is more of it.

"A doctor with a dirty mind, who fits a young woman with a diaphragm, can convince himself that there is a sexual explosion," he says. "He talks to the press in the role of marriage counselor, and then everyone else thinks so, too."

Mr. Gagnon says that the three most written about aspects of sexuality today are premarital relations, homosexuality, and the female orgasm. In his studies, Dr. Kinsey emphasized the orgasm. So do most marriage manuals. Because of this, says Dr. Robert R. Bell of Temple University, author of *Marriage and Family Interaction* and *Premarital Sex in a Changing Society*, too many brides are troubled when they are not carried away in a delirium of joy by one. "They expect the world to observe thirty seconds of silence when it first happens to them," he says.

Mrs. Ethel Nash, president of the American Association of Marriage Counselors, notes the emphasis on the female orgasm this way:

Twenty-five years ago, married couples visited marriage counselors and talked over their problems, which may or may not have been sexual. Later, wives came and said their husbands were sex maniacs, and what could they do about it? Now husbands come to talk about their wives' inability to have orgasms.

Mrs. Nash says that the question is no longer will she or won't she, but can she or can't she?

Dr. Catherine Chilman of the Department of Health, Education and Welfare says there is a "free-floating anxiety" about sexual perplexities and that "Americans are enchanted with finding new problems." Americans now imagine that there has been a sudden collapse of virtue, Dr. Chilman says. She disagrees with this, and the research supports her.

In *Factors in the Sex Life of Twenty-two Hundred Women,* which was published in 1929, Katherine B. Davis studied women who were in college in the early 1900's and concluded that only 7 percent had had premarital relations. The real change, sociologists say, came in the 1920's. In particular, it was the generation born between 1900 and 1910 that revolutionized American sexual behavior.

In *Psychological Factors in Marital Happiness,* published in 1938, Lewis M. Terman questioned a sample of 104 women born in the decade before 1890 and found that 86.5 percent were virgins when they were married. For 277 women born between 1890 and 1899 the figure was 74 percent, and for 336 women born between 1900 and 1909 it was 51.2 percent. Mr. Terman concluded from this that the virgin bride would disappear by 1960. He was wrong.

In *Premarital Dating Behavior* in 1959, Winston W. Ehrman said that only 13 percent of a sample of girls eighteen to twenty-two years old at a large coeducational university were not virgins. However, the presence of a larger number of the younger girls in the sample may have lowered the percentage.

The objection that is usually made to surveys of sexual behavior such as these is that it is only the middle class that is being surveyed, usually by middle-class professors. No one is ever quite sure what the very poor are doing, although most studies indicate that there is more permissiveness among them. However, there is also evidence that, as more youths attend college and as affluence spreads, middle-class morality becomes more pervasive.

In the *Merrill-Palmer Quarterly* last year, Mervin B. Freedman, who is now chairman of the psychology department at San Francisco State College, reported on a study at an Eastern women's college. The college, which was not identified, is generally considered advanced. Eighty of its freshmen were selected at random and then periodically were interviewed while they remained in college by four psychologists, a sociologist, and an anthropologist.

Most of the girls were from the upper middle class and about half were from the Middle Atlantic states. Some 70 percent were Protestant, 20 percent were Jewish, and 10 percent were Catholic. Twenty-nine of the girls left in the normal attrition of college years and two of those who remained refused to answer some of the questions they were asked. (The questions concerned family income, not sex. Similarly, some hygiene teachers say they can discuss sex, but not acne, with their students; pimples are too personal.) Of the forty-nine girls remaining in the study, eleven had had sexual relations by the time they were graduated. Eight of the eleven were involved in serious emotional relationships with their partners; three were not. Two of these three girls had relations with two men. None of the eleven expressed remorse.

The survey is consistent with the few other studies of sex and the student: they all say that great guilt does not accompany most premarital relationships, and they all put non-virginity among college women at 20 percent or less. Indeed, the question may be why, amidst otherwise sweeping social change, has the pattern of sexual activity apparently remained intact?

William Simon, another senior trustee at the Institute for Sex Research, suggests that perhaps American youth cannot afford the emotional investment that sex demands. However, Professor Freedman wrote:

Despite an appearance of worldliness and sophistication, it seems that conservatism, inhibition of impulse, cautiousness and willingness to defer gratification are part and parcel of American middle-class character.

A fair consensus of the psychologists, sociologists, marriage counselors, and other professionals in the field would show a feeling that Americans are developing new sex ethics, but little agreement on what those ethics might be. A few believe that Americans will someday accept what they call permissiveness without affection, which means that sexual relations will be acceptable among consenting adults even when there is no great emotional attachment. More, however, believe that America is moving toward an acceptance of what they call permissiveness with affection, which means that sex will be respectable among unmarried partners when there is mutual affection. They note that a pattern that may be developing among the young is engagement, followed by coitus, followed by marriage. Virtually every study that has been made of sexual behavior says that about half of all engaged couples are having relations. If there is a rise in any category of sexual activity, it is thought to be here.

The sociologists, psychologists, and marriage counselors also say that few youths can express an ethical argument either for or against premarital relations with any great conviction. This does not mean that promiscuity is likely to become rampant. In one survey of 253 unmarried sociology students in Iowa, only 59 percent of those who approved of a premarital relationship actually had experienced one.

In 1960, in *Premarital Sexual Standards in America,* Dr. Ira L. Reiss of the University of Iowa predicted that "the next 50 years, like the last 50 years, will witness an increasing acceptance of person-centered coitus and petting." Increasingly, he said, Americans will accept permissiveness with affection. Dr. Reiss has not changed his views on this. He notes that abstinence has lost its traditional supports, that the risk of pregnancy and venereal disease has lessened and that social condemnation and even guilt feelings are different now. Dr. Kinsey, for example, said that almost 90 percent of the women he interviewed had no real remorse about their premarital sexual behavior.

If a new sex ethic does develop, it may not be restricted by social class. Dr. Kinsey and his associates tended to consider each educational group a separate social class, and they said that less educated girls had intercourse five or six years earlier than girls with high-school or college educations. They also said that, at the age of twenty-five, only 10 percent of the unmarried men with eighth-grade educations had not had relations. For high-school graduates, they said, the figure was 16 percent and for college graduates it was 36 percent.

Dr. Kinsey was studying behavior, not attitudes, but the implication was that a drop-out was likely to feel less restrained about sex than an astrophysicist. However, Dr. Reiss, who has studied attitudes, not behavior, disagrees. In the *American Sociological Review,* he describes a survey of 903 single students and 1,515 adults. The students were from two high schools and three colleges in New York and Virginia. The adults, 80 percent of them unmarried, were chosen by the National Opinion Research Center and represent a national sample.

Dr. Reiss concluded that "people who share generally liberal or conservative attitudes are more likely to share similar attitudes toward sex than are people who merely earn the same salary or have gone to school the same number of years." It is the style of life that determines sexual attitudes, according to Dr. Reiss. What matters is being a fundamentalist or a Unitarian, preferring W. C. Fields to Jerry Lewis, or maybe Garbo to Elizabeth Taylor. "Social class," he writes, "seemed to have no real effect on permissiveness." This is particularly true, he says, in the upper social and economic reaches, "where permissiveness represents an underlying set of attitudes that vary independently of conventional indices of status."

For some, the fact that sex is being analyzed and discussed, that it is, in effect, going public, will rob it of enchantment. This is an area where poets and prudes can be agitated together, and perhaps nothing will agitate them as much as the recently published *Human Sexual Response,* by Dr. William H. Masters, a gynecologist, and Virginia E. Johnson, a psychologist. Before them, medical science had made few attempts to explore the physiology of sex. Freud and even Dr. Kinsey had to rely largely on what their subjects told them, and since the work of Dr. Robert Latou Dickinson, whose *Human Sex Anatomy* first appeared in 1933, little has appeared on the subject.

Mrs. Nash, who is an assistant professor at the Bowman Gray School of Medicine in Winston-Salem, N. C., as well as a marriage counselor, says that one great virtue of the Masters-Johnson research is that it can be used in counseling

to give people a real feeling of what is happening to them during intercourse. You can tell people they're not abnormal, that here is something they can look for. You can also tell them something about the difference in the frequency desires between men and women when things don't work out. For the merely naive, the book can be used to provide a primer on their own responses.

Dr. Masters and Mrs. Johnson, who are working at the Reproductive Biology Research Foundation in St. Louis, began a clinical program on the treatment of sexual inadequacy in 1959. They have not disclosed their results yet, but they say they are working on it together, using a team approach. They say that, in a marriage where there are problems of sexual inadequacy, both partners are involved, and they insist on complete cooperation from both of them. They coach the wife of the sexually inadequate husband in the physiologic and psychologic aspects of her husband's sexual response and then invite her to join the team. Similarly, a husband with an inadequate wife would be told about the female cycle of response, and then he would join.

This attempt to train someone in coitus is the last word in sexual therapy, and it is certain to be both hailed as the final sexual emancipation and excoriated as the final indignity. It is probably neither one nor the other, and its acceptance or rejection will tell a good deal about American sexual attitudes.

Suggestions for Further Reading

Historians have not written much about American sexuality in the twentieth century, except in passing. The book to begin study with is Sidney Ditzion, *Marriage, Morals, and Sex in America* (New York, 1953) which concentrates on the best known sexual radicals. It is descriptive rather than analytical. Paul S. Boyer, *Purity in Print: The Vice-Society Movement and Book Censorship in America* (New York, 1968) is an engrossing account that answers many questions about the censorship problem. David M. Kennedy, *Birth Control in America* (New Haven, 1970) focuses on the career of Margaret Sanger. William L. O'Neill, *Divorce in the Progressive Era* (New Haven, 1967) includes two chapters on the new moralists who helped undermine Victorian sexual standards. The only history of the family in America, Arthur W. Calhoun, *A Social History of the American Family* (Cleveland, 1919), is unfortunately much out of date. Volume III, *Since the Civil War,* is still worth reading, however, for the useful material it contains. The state of the art is discussed in Edward N. Saveth, "The Problem of American Family History," *American Quarterly* (Summer, 1969), pp. 311-29.

One subject that has attracted scholarly interest is prostitution. See the following: Egal Feldman, "Prostitution, the Alien Woman, and the Progressive Imagination," *American Quarterly* (Summer, 1967), pp. 192–206, Paul H. Hass, "Sin in Wisconsin: The Teasdale Vice Committee of 1913," *Wisconsin Magazine of History* (Winter, 1965), pp. 138–51, Roy Lubove, "The Progressive and the Prostitute," *The Historian* (May, 1962), pp. 308–30, Robert E. Riegel, "Changing American Attitudes Towards Prostitution," *Journal of the History of Ideas* (July-Sept., 1968), pp. 437-52, and the unpublished doctoral dissertation by Richard R. Wagner, *Virtue Against Vice: A Study of*

Moral Reformers and Prostitution in the Progressive Era (Wisconsin, 1971). The Progressive Era, the period from the late 1890s to World War I, has been the subject of much study because public anxiety over prostitution reached its peak during those years. The most complete study of prostitution in this century is Charles Winick and Paul M. Kinsie, *The Lively Commerce: Prostitution in the United States* (Chicago, 1971).

The published literature on sex is so enormous that it is practically impossible to represent it with the few titles that can be included here. The most complete bibliography on sex and related topics is Joan Aldous and Reuben Hill, *International Bibliography of Research in Marriage and the Family* (Minneapolis, 1967). The most direct way of establishing what was believed about sexuality at the turn of the century is to look at G. Stanley Hall's *Adolescence* (New York, 1904), which contains an incredible amount of misinformation. Thanks to Havelock Ellis and other students of sexuality the great tide of ignorance began to recede thereafter. Some useful material on the pioneers is to be found in Edward M. Brecher, *The Sex Researchers* (New York, 1971). A number of interesting studies were made during the 1920s, one of which is Katherine B. Davis, *Factors in the Sex Life of 2,200 Women* (New York, 1929). Her study was based on questionnaires sent to the graduates of women's colleges. Most of the respondents were over 30 at the time and it is instructive to compare their views with those of the young girls surveyed at almost the same time by Phyllis Blanchard and Carlyn Manasses, although the latter did not publish their book *New Girls for Old* (New York, 1937) until seven years later. Gilbert Van Tassel Hamilton, *A Research in Marriage* (New York, 1929) is absorbing because it is taken from extensive sessions with two hundred married people conducted by a psychiatrist. A good contemporary account of the revolution in morals during the 1920s is in Frederick Lewis Allen, *Only Yesterday* (New York, 1931), ch. 5. Other expressions, mostly of enthusiasm, about sexual freedom in this crucial period are V. F. Calverton and S. D. Schmalhausen, eds., *Sex in Civilization* (New York, 1929) and Frieda Kirchway, ed., *Our Changing Morality* (New York, 1924).

Public interest in sex declined rapidly after the crash in 1929. The principal piece of research in the 1930s is Lewis M. Terman, *Psychological Factors in Marital Happiness* (New York, 1938). Terman's data conformed to Kinsey's in that both showed women born after 1900 to have had significantly more pre-marital sex than those born earlier. Beginning in the 1940s with the first Kinsey report the literature becomes so abundant as to defy summary. A great deal was written about the two reports by Alfred Kinsey *et. al.*, *Sexual Behavior in the Human Male* (Philadelphia, 1948) and *Sexual Behavior in the Human Female* (Philadelphia, 1953). Among the more useful books are Albert Deutsch, ed., *Sex Habits of American Men: A Symposium on the Kinsey Report* (New York, 1948), Albert Ellis, ed., *Sex Life of the American Woman and the Kinsey Report* (New York, 1954), and Donald Porter Geddes, ed., *An Analysis of the Kinsey Reports on Sexual Behavior in the Human Male and Female* (New York, 1954). The two books by William H. Masters and Virginia E. Johnson *Human Sexual Response* (Boston, 1966) and *Human Sexual Inadequacy* (Boston, 1970) also generated a substantial literature. Much of it is not so much critical as explanatory since both books are almost unintelligible to laymen.

Hence the following: Ruth and Edward Brecher, eds., *An Analysis of Human Sexual Inadequacy,* an excerpt from which is included in this volume; Jhan and June Robbins, eds., *An Analysis of Human Sexual Inadequacy* (New York, 1970); and Nat Lehrman, ed., *Masters and Johnson Explained* (Chicago, 1970). The Lehrman book contains a fascinating interview with Masters and Johnson that was first published in *Playboy* magazine.

Current sexual topics have been explored in staggering detail. A good summary of current thinking is the *Annals* special issue "Sex and the Contemporary American Scene" (March, 1968). There is not much that is new where sexual behavior is concerned, an apparent exception being the rapid rise of mate swapping since the birth control pill was made available in 1960. This curiosity is described in Gilbert D. Bartell, *Group Sex* (New York, 1971). A number of recent books by feminists have discussed sexual problems from a woman's point of view. The best of them, I think, is Shulamith Firestone, *The Dialectic of Sex* (New York, 1970). It should be compared with a classic German feminist work that anticipates many current questions, Grete Meisel-Hess, *The Sexual Crisis* (New York, 1917).

As everyone knows, and the Commission on Pornography and Obscenity proved, pornography is not a very absorbing subject once the initial thrill is gone. Two books that manage to deal with it interestingly are Steven Marcus, *The Other Victorians* (New York, 1966) and Morse Peckham, *Art and Pornography* (New York, 1969).

A visit to any paperback bookstore will provide the average reader with more material on sex than he can handle in a lifetime.